Witness in a Pagan World

A Study of Mark's Gospel

by

Eric Johns and David Major

Lutterworth Press · Cambridge

Lutterworth Press
P.O. Box 60,
Cambridge CB1 2NT

British Library Cataloguing-in-Publication Data available

ISBN 0 7188 2480 6

First published 1980
Reprinted 1985, 1987, 1988

Printed in Great Britain by
The Guernsey Press Co. Ltd., Guernsey, Channel Islands.

Contents

Maps and Diagrams

Introduction

This book was written as a result of our experiences trying to help O-level and C.S.E. pupils to prepare for their examinations. Besides these people, however, we hope it will be of interest to the general reader and Bible student who wants to know more about Mark's gospel.

It was established in the nineteenth century that Mark was the first of the Synoptic Gospels to be written and was the source of much of the material in Matthew and Luke. It is, therefore, essential for our understanding of the Christian message to try to discover the influences to which Mark was exposed and how he responded to them.

Mark was a Christian witness in a pagan world and in many respects today's world is similar to his. The gospel then, as now, was frequently ignored or misunderstood and its witnesses persecuted. If such a situation is to be improved upon then openness and a critical understanding of basic Christian scriptures must be encouraged so that the gospel's relevance to people today may be discovered.

With this aim in view we have endeavoured to make available the latest theological scholarship in a form which, we hope, people will find both interesting and intelligible. The emphasis of this book is on Mark as a creative writer who was attempting to present the truth about Jesus, as he saw it, in a way which would make sense to his readers. This is the task which every generation of Christians undertakes and it is never finished.

The quotations used are from the New English Bible but the book can be read alongside any version of the Bible.

I

The background to the gospel

TIME CHART SHOWING EVENTS OF FIRST CENTURY AD

(Dates are approximate)

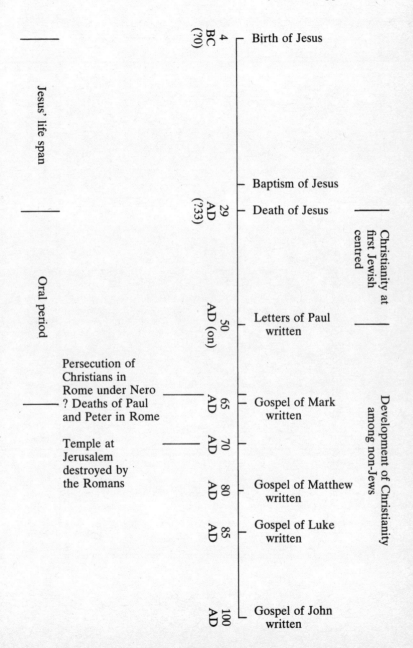

4 BC (?0)	Birth of Jesus
	Baptism of Jesus
AD 29 (?33)	Death of Jesus
AD 50 (on)	Letters of Paul written
65 AD	Gospel of Mark written
70 AD	
80 AD	Gospel of Matthew written
85 AD	Gospel of Luke written
100 AD	Gospel of John written

Jesus' life span

Oral period

Persecution of Christians in Rome under Nero ? Deaths of Paul and Peter in Rome

Temple at Jerusalem destroyed by the Romans

Christianity at first Jewish centred

Development of Christianity among non-Jews

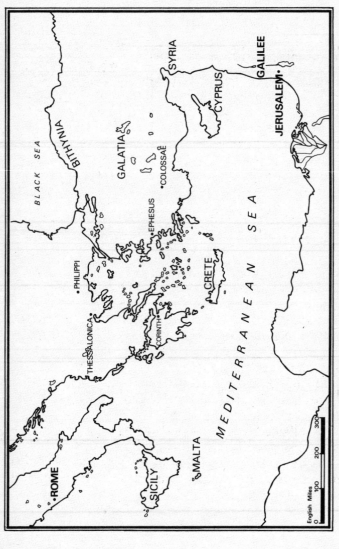

This map of the Mediterranean shows the positions of *Galilee* and *Jerusalem* where Jesus lived and died and *Rome* where Mark probably wrote his gospel a generation later. Also shown on the map are some of the places where churches were established by the time Mark wrote. In the New Testament we have Paul's letters to some of these churches.

1. What is a gospel?

a. The meaning of the word 'gospel'

The simplest way to begin to answer the question 'What is a gospel?' is to look at the history of the word 'gospel' itself and to see what it means.

Our word 'gospel' is made up of two Old English words 'god' and 'spell'. These words have been combined and shortened to give us the modern word 'gospel'. The word 'god' in Old English meant 'good', and the word 'spell' meant 'news' or 'story'. So the word 'gospel' means 'good news'.

We can trace the word back further than Old English. The Latin word is *evangelium* and from this we form our words 'evangelise' and 'evangelist'. Mark is an evangelist: that is, one who proclaims the gospel.

We can go back still one step further. The Latin is a translation of the Greek in which Mark's gospel and the New Testament were originally written. The Greek word for gospel is *euangelion*. Like the Old English this word also has two parts. The *eu* means 'good' and the *angelion* means 'news' or 'message'. It can be seen that when the translation into Old English was made, the words which came to form our word 'gospel' reflected very accurately the meaning of the original Greek.

If 'gospel' means 'good news' the next question which needs an answer is: What is this good news?

This is the question we shall be trying to answer in the rest of this book. But to give you a brief answer – it is the good news about Jesus.

b. The oral period and the expectation of the Second Coming

(i) How the message was proclaimed

Jesus was crucified sometime during the years AD 29–33. Mark wrote his gospel about AD 65. The period between these two events is called the 'oral period'. This simply means the time when the gospel was passed on by word of mouth.

Jesus had been a wandering preacher. He had travelled through Galilee and Judaea and the surrounding areas preaching the good news. He taught congregations in synagogues, spoke to crowds of people in the towns and countryside, and instructed his closest disciples in small groups.

When, after Jesus' death, his followers came to decide how they should continue his work, it was natural for them to choose the same methods as their master. These methods were also the most efficient, for until the invention of printing the quickest way to spread news was by speaking directly to crowds of people. Writing on papyrus scrolls was slow and, in a world where very many people could not read, it was not an effective way of spreading urgent news.

Jesus himself had left no written teaching. He made up stories and rhythmical sayings which were easy to remember, and his disciples followed the custom of the time by memorising them. There was little danger of their forgetting the gospel message because it was not written down; people who rarely use writing have far better memories than those of us brought up to make a note of everything we are told.

During the oral period the methods and example of Jesus guided the Christian missionaries as they proclaimed the gospel. There were Jewish communities in very many cities in the countries bordering the Mediterranean Sea. On Sabbath days the missionaries proclaimed the good news in the synagogues in these cities. At other times they stood in the city square and argued with passers-by or with the pagan priests. But when anyone, Jew or Gentile, showed an interest in their message they taught them in small groups and prepared them for baptism.

The missionaries converted people in cities all round the Mediterranean. Once a group was established they moved on and preached the gospel elsewhere, for there was no time to lose. By this means, in a very few years, Christianity spread through the most populous part of the Roman Empire.

This was a great achievement for the missionaries, but the question which follows from this is: Why did they consider the gospel to be so urgent?

(ii) Why the good news was urgent

In the last section we mentioned three reasons why the gospel message was not at first written down.

First, Jesus himself had not left any written teaching. Second, it was the custom among the Jews who became the first followers of Jesus to memorise a teacher's words not to write them down. Third, in those days writing was a slow way to spread news and the message was urgent.

The last reason is the most important.

The first Christians believed they were living at a very remarkable time. They thought that God had a three-stage plan for the world. The first stage had been the time of the Old Testament. During this period God had rescued the Israelites, his chosen people, from Egypt, and sent his prophets to reveal his plan to them alone. That stage had ended when Jesus had appeared on earth. He was the Messiah whom the prophets had promised and his lifetime was the second stage of the world's history.

The third stage was the period they were now living in. Like the second stage it was only to be brief, shorter than their own lifetime. They believed that, after being crucified and raised from the dead, Jesus was only waiting for the moment when he was to return and bring the world to an end. This event is known as the Second Coming. The exact moment when Jesus would return had been chosen by God and that moment had almost arrived.

The first Christians saw themselves as people with a vitally important message and only a brief time in which to deliver it. (Look up 13:10 and 13:30.) When Jesus returned, those who had faith in him would be rewarded with a life of bliss in a perfect kingdom ruled by Jesus himself. Those who did not believe would perish. There was to be no second chance for anyone who could not make up his mind. You had to choose: you were either for Jesus or against him.

If you were a Christian missionary you stood up in the

9

market place and told people the good news. If they did not believe you, then you were to do as Jesus had taught, 'Shake the dust off your feet as you leave, as a warning to them' (6:11). Then you hurried on to the next town. The gospel could not wait.

(iii) The good news in the oral period

What did missionaries say to the people whom they wished to convert to Christianity? We can find some clues to the answer if we look at the stories and incidents recorded in Mark's gospel.

The first thing we have to remember is that for Christians Jesus was not dead. He had been crucified but he had risen from the dead; now he was in heaven ruling the universe and waiting for the moment when he would return to earth. So the missionaries had first of all to explain that someone who had died on the cross was alive.

For Christians this was the most amazing event in the history of the world – but it was not unexpected. If you knew the place to look you would see that it was all part of God's plan, and that his prophets had foretold everything. That place was the Old Testament, the holy book of the Jews.

In the ancient world the Jews were regarded with both respect and fear. They possessed one of the oldest books known to man and, because of this, they were believed to have knowledge of things hidden from other people. Christian missionaries told their audiences that everything which had happened to Jesus had been written down in the past in the Jewish Bible, and they backed up this claim by quoting words from the Old Testament prophets. Mark begins his gospel by making use of several of these prophecies (see chapter 5).

Many of those who heard the missionaries wanted to become Christians. As soon as that happened questions sprang to mind and they needed to be taught about their new religion, much as people who are going to be confirmed are taught today. It was the needs of these people which often decided the way in which the good news was remembered.

Christianity first of all was a religion of the poorer, often uneducated members of society. Paul says, 'Few of you are

10

men of wisdom, by any human standard; few are powerful or highly born' (1 Cor. 1:26). So the teaching given to the new Christians had to be easy to remember and understand.

In Mark's gospel you will find parables, miracle stories, sayings of Jesus, accounts of people in contact with him, and the account of his death and resurrection. Much of this was easy for an ordinary person to remember. For example, if the new Christian wanted to know what the kingdom of God was like, then the parable of the mustard seed could be told (4:30–32). Everyone can remember a story without difficulty.

The miracle stories were remembered by the church because they showed the power of Jesus. They revealed to those able to understand them that Jesus worked with God's authority. Again these were quite easy to remember. There was no more detail in each story than was absolutely necessary. (Look up 1:21–28 for an example.)

The sayings of Jesus, though, were not so easy to remember, and to make things simpler those which had something in common were gathered together. For example, sayings in which the word 'salt' appeared were placed one after the other. In this way, when one saying was recalled the rest sprang to mind. (Look up 9:49–50 for three sayings linked in this way.)

Other sayings were attached to short stories which helped to explain their meaning. This also made them easier to remember. One example is the saying, 'Pay Caesar what is due to Caesar, and pay God what is due to God.' The story which goes with it is remembered mainly because it leads up to the saying or *pronouncement* of Jesus. It is therefore called a Pronouncement Story (12:13–17).

The incidents from Jesus' life could be remembered as easily as stories, but the only details people bothered to repeat were those which taught them something. The early Christians were not interested in a day by day biography of Jesus. If they wanted to know why they had to be baptised, then the story of Jesus' baptism would be told to help them understand the meaning of the ceremony they underwent to become Christians (1:9–11).

It was the same with the accounts of people who came into contact with Jesus. Christians asked what there was to be learned from the event. They were not interested in the people for any other reason. In the story of the call of Levi all that was important was that he followed Jesus *immediately* (2:14). That showed how they themselves should respond to Jesus' call. We learn next to nothing about Levi himself.

To sum up, we can say that the members of the early church influenced the preaching of the good news in two ways.

First, the sort of people they were decided the *way* the gospel was preached. Second, what they needed to know decided *what* was preached.

Much of the teaching from the oral period has been written down in the gospels. How Mark made use of this teaching we shall examine in chapter 4.

c. Why the good news was written down

If you look in the New Testament you will find four gospels. Since the good news was at first passed on by word of mouth the question we ask is: When and why did Christians begin to write the books we now call gospels?

Christian teachings were probably first written down during the oral period. We should not imagine that the oral period ended abruptly and that the period of written records began immediately afterwards. The oral and written traditions ran side by side for a long time.

It is possible that before Mark wrote his gospel there were shorter, less detailed Christian writings. They probably recorded some sayings of Jesus or the account of his last days and death. It is very difficult to be sure that such writings existed because no copies have survived the centuries. Scholars study the gospels, and at certain places they say that it looks as though just here Mark or Matthew or Luke copied from some earlier account.

Mark's gospel is the oldest full-length gospel we have. It was written about AD 65. So we can say that within a generation of the death of Jesus some Christians thought it necessary to put a connected account of the good news into writing.

What was happening which led to this?

1. Jesus' original disciples were growing old. By the time

Mark wrote, those who were still alive must have been over sixty and probably over seventy, a good age for those times.

This meant that those who had known Jesus and been taught by him were a dying band. It was not only old age which had reduced their numbers but also persecution. As early as AD 42 James, the brother of John, had been killed (Acts 12:2). In AD 64 Peter and Paul were probably killed in Rome during the Emperor Nero's persecution of Christians.

The remaining disciples were scattered about the churches of the Mediterranean world. They proclaimed the gospel and taught the faithful to the best of their ability. Each of them made use of the parts of Jesus' teaching which made the gospel clear to members of his church, and as people vary so did the parts they chose to use.

The result was that no one church knew all the stories about Jesus or all his teaching. As the original disciples died there was a danger that first-hand knowledge of Jesus' work would die with them. There would be no one to turn to in order to check that the teaching had been understood correctly. People began to feel that it would be safer to write down the good news.

2. Time was passing and there was no sign of the Second Coming of Jesus. Christians began to wonder whether they had misunderstood what Jesus had taught. Perhaps the Second Coming was not after all to be in their own lifetime. As this idea spread, people felt a need to examine more carefully what Jesus had taught. Mark wrote his gospel to make clear what the good news really meant.

3. When a church was persecuted and its members killed or scattered, there was a danger that some precious part of the gospel would be lost for ever. It then became urgent to set it down and to send copies to other churches to save that church's part of the gospel.

4. When Christians met for worship they followed the Jewish tradition of reading from the Old Testament. It was natural to wish to have readings about the deeds and words of Jesus himself. This need would be especially felt as the number of people who knew him and could retell the stories grew less.

These are some of the reasons for the ending of the oral period. What followed was the period of written records in which we still live.

d. A gospel is not a biography

There have been many attempts to write a biography of Jesus but none has been successful. The reason for this is very simple. We do not have the sort of information about Jesus necessary to construct a modern biography.

The categories we use to classify different types of books – history, fiction, poetry, biography and so on – were not so strict in the first century AD. For example, history books could be written in verse, fact and fiction mixed together, and biographies used to teach lessons in correct behaviour.

Mark lived in a very different world from ours and when he wrote he put in his book what he thought important. He was not writing a biography as we should today, and if we list the information which is missing we can see this clearly.

We do not know about Jesus' childhood in Nazareth, nor about his youth, nor how he spent the years before his baptism by John. We do not even know whether he was married, although we suppose not. We do not know his height, nor the colour of his eyes, nor the year of his birth, nor the year of his death. We do not even know the order of events during the years of his teaching which the gospels describe.

To find out why Mark left out all this information we have to remind ourselves what interested the early church.

The church was in a hurry to spread the good news. When people became Christians they needed to know what Jesus had taught and how they ought to live. The order of events in Jesus' life was not important. Once you believed that Jesus was the Messiah promised by the Old Testament you wanted to know what he had said and to understand the signs he had given.

If you asked whether you should pay Roman taxes then the saying, 'Pay Caesar what is due to Caesar, and pay God what is due to God,' was what you needed to hear. It did not matter whether Jesus had said it in Galilee or Jerusalem, before the feeding of the five thousand or after it. The teaching was all that mattered.

The early church did not bother to keep a record of the order of events. It taught the things which helped Christians in their own lives.

The biographer wants to know what Jesus looked like. To the early Christians such knowledge would have seemed useless. It was your response to his teaching which mattered. Besides, when Jesus returned he would be in a new, radiant body.

The gospel therefore is not a modern biography. It does not set out to describe Jesus and his daily life. Its aim is to tell the good news.

Questions for chapter 1

1. What does the word 'gospel' mean?

2. Why did the early Christians think that the gospel message was urgent?

3. What led the early Christians to write down the good news?

4. Why is a gospel not the same as a biography of Jesus?

2. Who was Mark?

a. A Christian in Rome?

This book is about Mark's gospel, but how much do we really know about this Mark who gave his name to the gospel? We know only his Christian name and we possess no personal details about him, but we are still able to find out a few things. There are three sources of information we can use.

First, there is the gospel itself. By studying it we can work out what views he held and make a good guess about the sort of people he wrote for. Second, we can look for any mention of him which occurs elsewhere in the New Testament. Lastly, we can examine any documents not in the New Testament which mention him or his gospel.

(i) Clues to Mark's identity in his gospel

When people read the gospels they often think that the writer was present at the events he describes, and that he was jotting down what happened rather like a reporter today. Mark does not claim to have known Jesus and he never once says 'I' in his gospel. Some commentators on Mark have suggested that he was the unnamed young man who ran away when Jesus was arrested (14:51–52). Although this is an attractive idea, there is nothing to suggest that he was or that he knew Jesus personally.

Mark's gospel begins and ends abruptly. He wrote in Greek, but his is not the polished language of an educated man. His style is rough and ready and sometimes ungrammatical. It drives home its message forcefully, and that message is not a gentle one.

He appears to be writing for people who took a great risk when they became Christians. He makes it plain that Christians must expect opposition, and he emphasises the opposition Jesus met. His description of Jesus' suffering and death is the harshest in the New Testament.

16

This style of writing would help people who were themselves suffering. It would make their suffering understandable and give them the strength to bear it. This suggests that he was a member of one of the churches which was suffering persecution.

(ii) The name 'Mark' in the New Testament

Do the other books in the New Testament help us to identify Mark or his church?

The first thing we must note is that 'Mark' (Latin *Marcus*) was one of the commonest names of the Roman Empire. There were probably many Christians with that name, so whenever we come across any mention of someone called Mark we should not automatically assume that the person referred to is the gospel writer.

This is what the early Christians did. The result was that once the name Mark was attached to the gospel the author was identified with anyone else called Mark who appeared in the New Testament. For centuries it was believed that there was only one Mark – the person who wrote the gospel, was mentioned in Paul's letters, appeared in the Acts of the Apostles, and is referred to at the end of the first letter of Peter.

We cannot be absolutely certain, but it seems unlikely that the Mark of Acts and Paul's letters is the author of the gospel. The Mark who accompanied Paul is called John Mark in Acts and his mother, we are told, had a house in Jerusalem. If this was the evangelist's home it would explain his crude Greek. He would, like other missionaries have spoken Greek, but his native language would have been Aramaic.

The argument against Jerusalem being his home is that the Mark who wrote the gospel does not seem to know the geography of Palestine. At 7:31 he describes one of Jesus' journeys. If you look at the map on page 39 you will see that it is almost impossible to plot the route which goes all over the place. Someone who knew the region would have tried to make it fit in with the geography of the country.

Even if someone living in Jerusalem was ignorant of towns in northern Palestine he would have known the Jerusalem area. But when Mark describes Jesus' approach to Jerusalem from Jericho the towns he passes through are given in the wrong order. Again this would be a strange thing for someone who knew the area to do (11:1). For these reasons we think it unlikely that this Mark wrote the gospel.

There is another mention of the name Mark in the New Testament. In 1 Peter 5:13 someone called Mark is said to be with the letter-writer in Babylon. 'Babylon' was a name given by Christians to Rome. It meant a place of evil. If the writer really was Peter (and we cannot even be sure of that!) then it is possible that the Mark referred to was the author of the gospel.

To see why this might be so we have to bring in evidence from outside the New Testament.

(iii) Information from outside the New Testament

In about AD 320 Eusebius, Bishop of Caesarea, wrote a history of the church. In it he quoted Papias, who was the Bishop of Hierapolis in about AD 130, and who had reported what an elder of the church used to say. This elder said that Mark was the interpreter of Peter. That is, he was taught by Peter and later wrote down what he remembered.

Papias is believed to have emphasised Mark's connection with Peter in order to put the authority of this gospel beyond question. He wanted to do this because he was in dispute with Christians who, he thought, had strayed from Christ's teachings. We must, therefore, be careful how much trust we put in what he wrote. There are, however, other reasons for thinking that Peter may have been connected with this gospel.

1. Peter is presented by Mark as being very human and weak. It is the sort of opinion a modest man might hold of himself and pass on to someone he taught.

2. If Peter was martyred in Rome in AD 64 at the time of the Emperor Nero's persecution of Christians, his death might have been the spur which made Mark write. The Roman historian, Tacitus, described the treatment of Christians at this time in these words, 'They were clad in the hides of beasts and torn to death by dogs; others were crucified, others set on fire to serve to illuminate the night when daylight failed.' Mark emphasised the suffering which a Christian might expect and if he was writing for a church

18

being persecuted, as the one in Rome was, that would be understandable.

3. Mark's gospel became widely known very quickly and was accepted as an accurate account of the good news. If it was composed in Rome then the city's connection with Peter and Paul would have given it authority in Christian eyes. (See chapter 3 b. and c. for Peter and Paul's influence on Mark.)

4. There is a tradition in the church which has always connected Mark's gospel with Rome. We must treat tradition cautiously, but it can be a useful source of information especially when there is other evidence which supports it.

In answer to the question with which we started this chapter, we should say that Mark was a member of a persecuted church, that it was somewhere in the Gentile world, and that most probably it was in Rome.

b. When was the gospel written?

Deciding who Mark was also helps to decide the date when the gospel was written. The date usually given is about AD 65. There are four main arguments in favour of this date.

1. According to Papias, Mark wrote what he *remembered* of Peter's teaching. If Peter had still been there he could have asked him for details, and no doubt a different sort of book would have been the result. It seems that by the time Mark wrote Peter was probably dead which, if he died under Nero, means that Mark wrote after AD 64.

2. The tone of the gospel, as we have noted, suggests that Mark wrote for people experiencing persecution. If Mark wrote in Rome this again suggests a date soon after AD 64 when that church was being persecuted.

3. Both Matthew and Luke, when they wrote their gospels, made use of Mark's gospel. Most commentators believe that they wrote before the end of the first century, and since they did not live in Rome we have to allow time for Mark's work to be copied and distributed and for its authority to be widely accepted. We can say that AD 75

would be the latest date for Mark and still leave time for these things to happen.

4. It has been suggested that Mark wrote before the Jewish revolt and defeat by the Romans. The revolt started in AD 66 and Jerusalem was captured in AD 70. At 13:2 Mark records a prophecy which foretells the destruction of the temple in Jerusalem. As a result of the revolt the temple was destroyed by the Romans. If Mark wrote after this event, it is argued, then he would have made the prophecy apply more precisely to it.

This fits in with the AD 65 date, but we still cannot be sure. Mark may have been writing while the revolt was still in progress. In which case he would not have known the result although it could have been guessed at. Then again he could have written later and simply put down the prophecy or the bare facts as he had heard them. These are only suggestions and we have to be very careful not to put too much trust in them.

The most we can say is that Mark very likely wrote between AD 65 and 75. Whether you think it was early or late in that decade depends on how much weight you attach to the different pieces of evidence. But remember – the evidence is not conclusive.

Questions for chapter 2

1. What can we learn about Mark's readers from the way in which he wrote?

2. What evidence is there to suggest that Mark lived in Rome?

3. At what date do you think Mark's gospel was written?

3. Where did Mark find his material?

Where did Mark find the material he put in his gospel? He was not present at the events he describes so he must have had sources from which he drew his information. We have already mentioned two of these (the oral tradition and Peter) and there are two others – the Old Testament and Paul.

a. The oral tradition

Mark's first and most important source was the oral tradition of the early church. This was the teaching of the missionaries which was developed as the church expanded and was adapted to meet the needs of the new Christians. (The oral period is described in detail in chapter 1 b.)

Mark's church, like every other, had a collection of material which was the gospel of that particular church. This included the following types of material: parables, healing and miracle stories, sayings of Jesus, pronouncement stories, stories about Jesus and about people connected with him, and the story of his death and resurrection.

Mark used the oral tradition of his church as one of his sources and included this variety of material in his gospel.

b. Papias claimed Peter was Mark's source

We have already mentioned Papias and the elder who supplied him with information about Mark. This is what he had to say:

> The Elder used to say this also: Mark became the interpreter of Peter and he wrote down accurately, but not in order, as much as he remembered of the sayings and doings of Christ. For he was not a hearer or a follower of the Lord, but afterwards, as I said, of Peter, who adapted his teachings to the needs of the moment and did

not make an ordered exposition of the sayings of the Lord.

If Mark did obtain his information from Peter we should expect his gospel to contain accounts of events which only Peter would have known about, or to reflect a point of view we should expect him to hold.

We can see if this is so by listing some of the incidents in which Peter plays a part. Mark shows him being called Satan (8:33), being terrified and not knowing what to say (9:5–6), disowning Jesus three times (14:66–72), but still being mentioned by name in the message Jesus sent after his resurrection (16:7).

The picture of Peter painted by Mark is not flattering. It is the sort of portrait a modest man, someone who thought himself unworthy of his master, would paint of himself. So it is possible that Mark was faithfully recording what Peter had told him.

The disciples too are presented in a poor light. Mark must have had good reason to present both Peter and them so unfavourably. One possible solution to the puzzle is offered by Papias – that Peter was Mark's source.

But we must as usual add a caution. Much of Mark's gospel comes from the oral tradition, and it is possible that what looks to us like material which might have come directly from Peter was itself a part of that tradition. Those events of which we should expect Peter to have special knowledge (e.g. his denial of Jesus) could have been passed on by him to other disciples and so become a part of the teaching of the early church. Or, again, Peter may have taught at Rome and influenced the oral tradition of that church, and Mark may then have made use of it.

There is another possibility. Mark was writing for a persecuted church. In difficult times people find it hard to remain faithful, so Mark would aim in his writing to encourage his fellow Christians. One way to do this would be to emphasise the failings of the disciples. If Jesus could choose such people to be his closest companions, then there was hope for Mark's readers when in their turn they failed to keep faith with their master.

Taking all these points into account it seems likely that Mark had Peter's authority, either directly or through the oral tradition, for much of what he wrote. *But it was his own situation which decided for him what themes he should emphasise.*

c. Mark makes use of Paul's ideas

Paul, like Peter, is believed to have been executed in Rome in about AD 64. It is very likely that, if Mark belonged to the Christian church in Rome, he would have met Paul or had Paul's teaching passed on to him. In his gospel there are several themes which suggest that Paul may have been one of Mark's sources.

1. One belief they share is that grief in the face of death shows a lack of faith. If Jesus rose from the dead then so will his faithful followers. In the story of Jairus' daughter (5:21–43), Jesus instructs Jairus to have faith and wants to know why there is crying and commotion as the girl is only asleep. The story reflects Christian belief about death – it was only a sleep until Jesus should return.

In his letter to the Thessalonians, Paul says that he would not have them grieve for their brothers who were asleep (dead). The only ones who grieved were those who had no hope (pagans). If you had faith in Jesus, death was not the end because Christians would rise as Jesus had done.

2. The theme of death and resurrection is emphasised by both Mark and Paul. Mark begins his gospel with the baptism of Jesus. Baptism was a symbol: it signified the death of the old, pagan self and the birth of a new, Christian self. It also symbolised the death and resurrection of Jesus and the promise to his followers that they would be reborn in the kingdom of God.

Paul makes the point even more strongly. In his letter to the Romans (6:3) he says that Christians are baptised into Jesus' death so that they will be able to enjoy a resurrection like his. These beliefs made it possible for Christians to bear the hostility of the pagan world, and both Mark and Paul write to encourage Christians facing danger.

3. In his letters, Paul shows little interest in the life of Jesus; he usually refers to Jesus' death and resurrection. This event is the one which Paul believed to be the most

important. It showed the conquest of death which meant the conquest of evil, because death was evil's final triumph.

Jesus' resurrection was used by Paul to encourage Christians to face all the evils of this life – even to risk being martyred – confident that since Jesus had conquered death he would ensure their resurrection too.

In Mark there is a similar emphasis on the conquest of evil. One third of the gospel is devoted to stories of the miracles Jesus performed, and the majority of these show him conquering evil. The message from Paul and from Mark is the same: do not fear evil – Jesus has conquered it.

In spite of their agreement, it is very difficult to be absolutely certain that Mark made use of Paul. Paul may have influenced the Roman church and so have influenced Mark. Another possibility which could account for their agreement is that they lived at the same time. It may be that where they seem to be saying the same things it is simply that many Christians of their generation held the same beliefs.

d. The Old Testament

(i) Why the early Christians used the Old Testament

There can be no doubt that the Old Testament was one of Mark's sources. He makes use of it throughout his gospel.

When we look at Christianity today we see a world-wide religion with millions of followers. But when it started it was simply a tiny fragment of the religion of Judaism. It was not until about AD 45 that it became an independent religion. Beginning in this way it is not surprising that Christianity absorbed many Jewish ideas. We must remember too that Jesus was a Jew, and as such would have been thoroughly familiar with the Old Testament.

When the Christian religion was just beginning to spread across the Mediterranean region, there was no New Testament for the new converts to turn to. All the information they had about Jesus was the preaching of the missionaries. They did have a book though, and this was the Old Testament, the Bible of the Jews.

Both Jews and Christians believed that in it God had foretold, through the prophets, what his plans were for the world. Jews and Christians, however, did not agree about the meaning of all the prophecies. They agreed that God intended to send a Messiah, one appointed to be his representative on earth, but they disagreed about what the Messiah would do.

Some Jews expected a Messiah who would be a national hero, rebuild King David's empire, and get rid of the Romans. The Christians said that the Messiah had already lived, that he had been recognised by only a few people, that he had been a man of peace, and that he had suffered for the good of all mankind. Jesus was that Messiah.

When Jews and Christians argued about whether Jesus was the Messiah, the Christians quoted Old Testament prophecies to prove that he was and to show that everything that had happened to him was written there. Lists of prophecies were probably drawn up for Christians to use.

If a Christian teacher – like Mark, for instance – wished to explain why Jesus had died like a criminal, he turned to the Old Testament for an explanation. There he found records of how God's messengers had always suffered, and prophecies that God's plan for mankind would be achieved through innocent suffering.

(ii) The influence of the Old Testament on Mark

There was another result of using the Old Testament. When Christian writers got to work they knew it so well that they often wrote in a similar style. The words, the symbols and the images they used were those of the Old Testament, so that to understand them we have to understand the Old Testament.

Mark was no exception to this. From the very beginning of his gospel he makes use of Old Testament prophecy, language and ideas. He knows the Old Testament so well, and uses its terms so naturally, that in places it is difficult to say whether he is using it deliberately or whether it is simply second nature to him. As we go on we shall see how the Jewish Old Testament came to influence the Christian New Testament.

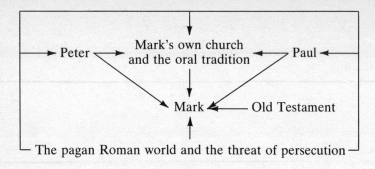

Diagram showing the influences which affected Mark as he wrote his gospel

Questions for chapter 3

1. Why is it likely that Mark had Peter for a source?

2. What themes do Paul and Mark have in common?

3. What was the holy book of the early Christians? How do you account for this?

4. The good news of Jesus as told by Mark

a. Mark the editor

In the last chapter we saw where Mark found the material he included in his gospel. In this chapter we want to try to discover how he made use of this material.

When Mark sat down to write he was not like a secretary simply copying down what his sources dictated to him. He was more like a newspaper editor selecting the most important stories to go into his account of the good news, and presenting them in a way which would make sense to his readers.

The question we must ask is: How did he decide what was important? To answer this we have to know two things: first, how his situation influenced him; and second, what he was aiming to do by arranging his material as he did.

b. What influenced Mark?

(i) The period in which he was living

We have to remember at all times that Mark wrote in the first century AD. We have already mentioned that the idea of a biography at that period was not the same as ours today, and that Mark was not a biographer.

Another mistake is to imagine that Mark worked like a modern historian. He did not set about his task by saying to himself that he must collect evidence from eye-witnesses and take care not to miss out or alter the minutest piece of information about Jesus' life. He was not really concerned with what an eye-witness would have seen. After all only those eye-witnesses who realised that Jesus was the Messiah would have really understood – really 'seen' – what was happening. The others, like the Pharisees, were 'blind' and so were not reliable witnesses.

Mark believed that it was his duty to make it absolutely

clear that Jesus was the Messiah – even if eye-witnesses had not been able to see this.

A good example of Mark at work is the baptism of Jesus. He believed that from the time of his baptism Jesus had been filled with the Holy Spirit. He wanted to show how this was accomplished, so he turned to the Old Testament to find a description of how God worked, and he used the images he found there to construct a picture of the baptism.

According to Mark the heavens were torn open, the Spirit, like a dove, descended and there was a voice from heaven. If these events had been seen and heard by everyone present there could have been no doubt about who Jesus was. But this was not the case. People did not immediately recognise him as the Messiah. What Mark's description does is to tell his readers that from the time of his baptism Jesus was the Messiah.

This is the point he wishes to make, and to make it is far more important than to record what imperfect human eyes saw. At the time Mark wrote there was no objection to him using his material in this way. What he was doing was writing a religious book, and he was influenced in the way he went about it by the opinions of the time.

(ii) The beliefs of Mark's time

We all have a set of beliefs which influence us but which we rarely think about. Mark was no exception to this rule. But can we say what he believed? What picture of the universe did he hold?

In the first century AD man's knowledge was very limited. He had no science in the way we have. The most important source of information for Mark and other Christians or Jews was the Bible. When they wondered about the universe they turned to the Bible and read about creation and God's purpose for mankind.

The view of the universe they held can be summarised as follows:

1. God created the world and all living creatures.
2. Throughout history, as recorded in the Old Testament, God had urged man in the direction which would fulfil his purpose in creating the world.

3. But man had often preferred to follow the path suggested by the powers of evil which opposed God.
4. At some time there would be a final battle between God and the powers of evil in which God would inevitably be triumphant, and his purpose would be fulfilled.
5. After this victory a certain number of people would be chosen by God to live in his presence in eternal bliss.
6. Lastly, and Christians alone believed this, the final battle had already been fought and won by Jesus who was the Messiah.

Mark held many other beliefs (for example, that evil spirits could cause illness) but they all fitted into this grand scheme for the universe which the Bible revealed. Everything he wrote had to fit in this scheme for the universe otherwise it would simply be nonsense.

(iii) The place Mark lived

In chapter 2 we suggested that Mark most likely belonged to the church at Rome. What we want to examine now is how this affected him when he wrote.

If you have ever written a letter you know that what you say depends on the person you are writing to. For example, if you are writing to someone who is ill you offer encouragement and probably say how good modern medicine is. We can see from his gospel that Mark is doing just this sort of thing.

His community was suffering persecution and this led him to write in a certain way. The people he was writing for were always in his thoughts as he chose his material and emphasised certain points. He certainly did not write for people living nearly two thousand years later.

He tried to explain his church's suffering and to encourage his fellow Christians. Suffering is a recurring theme in Mark and we shall examine it as we look at his aims.

c. Mark's aims as editor

Mark was writing for people who already believed that Jesus was the Messiah and the Son of God. He was not trying to convert anyone. He had other aims, and we can see from his gospel that they fall into three main groups.

1. He wanted to show that Jesus had been the Messiah during the whole of his ministry and not only after his resurrection. He also wanted to explain most people's failure to realise this when Jesus was alive and visible to them.

2. The popular Jewish picture of the Messiah, before and at the time of Jesus, was of a victorious military leader. Mark aimed to show how Jesus was victorious, not in a military sense, but in his battle with evil, and that his suffering and crucifixion were not the defeat they appeared to be, but a part of God's plan.

3. Mark wanted to explain how it was that the Messiah's followers appeared to be deserted by God and were allowed to suffer at the hands of pagans.

We can see how Mark went about his task as editor if we look at how he fulfilled each of his aims.

(i) Jesus the unrecognised Messiah

It must have been difficult for the early Christians to have understood how Jesus' real identity as the Messiah could have been hidden from most of the people who met him.

Mark reasoned that since Jesus had been sent to fulfil God's plan, if people failed to recognise him as the Messiah then that too must have been a part of the plan. God had caused the blindness, Mark believed, because he had wanted Jesus' true identity to remain a *secret* until such time as it suited his purpose to *reveal* it.

Mark also believed that Jesus had been the Messiah from the time of his baptism. The early Christians had not always thought this. To start with many of them seem to have believed that it was only after Jesus' death that God chose him to be his Messiah (see Rom. 1:2–4). As the years passed the belief grew in the church that Jesus had always been the Messiah, though the old idea still lingered on even after Mark's time.

According to Mark, Jesus did not claim publicly to be the Messiah until the very end of his life. It was only then that the secret was revealed. But it had always been possible for those who had faith to penetrate the secret. Jesus fulfilled the prophecies which had been made about the Messiah.

He cast out demons and healed the sick. By these signs (miracles) he told those who had faith who he really was.

Why does Mark emphasise secrecy? We can suggest three reasons.

1. If Jesus had openly accepted the title 'Messiah' it would have been thought that he intended to be a military leader come to re-establish an empire for the Jews. But he had a new idea of Messiahship, and to follow it he needed to be free from the warlike demands of patriots.

2. In Mark's time there were many pagan religions and each claimed to possess the only true knowledge of the gods. They kept their knowledge secret from all who were not members of their religion, and believed themselves to have a special relationship with their god or gods. Christians, such as Mark, lived in this sort of religious atmosphere and were influenced by it. They saw themselves as a part of God's plan. They were some of the few who would be chosen at the end of time to live in eternal bliss. The ones to be saved were those who really heard what Jesus said and really understood what the signs meant. To all the rest – those whom God had made blind – the parables and signs were mysteries (see 4:10–12 for an example). The key to them was faith in Jesus. If you did not have faith you could not understand and were not intended to: faith was what saved you.

3. Mark lived in a persecuted community. The secrecy about Jesus' Messiahship set an example of how the members of his church should live.

They had to meet and worship in secret because they were misunderstood, just as Jesus would have been if he had revealed himself. He had been forced to guard the truth about himself and so must they. If they revealed their beliefs they put themselves and their fellow Christians in danger. The powers of evil, in the form of the pagan authorities of their city, were still trying to stop the fulfilment of God's plan. They would go to any lengths to prevent the final triumph of good, so it became the duty of every Christian to keep silent.

In Mark's gospel it is only at the end of Jesus' life, when he is accused of being the Messiah by the High Priest, that he admits his true identity. This perhaps showed how the members of Mark's church declared their faith if, in their turn, they were caught and brought before their accusers, and could no longer hide their identity as followers of Jesus.

(ii) A Messiah of love and suffering

Mark's second aim as editor was to show how Jesus' idea of Messiahship differed from the traditional Jewish one.

At the time of Jesus, expectations of the Messiah's arrival were high among the Jews. They felt that the time must be near when God would send a great leader who would carve out a new Jewish kingdom by military conquest. If Jesus had started to talk about himself as the Messiah then he could not have followed the path he saw himself destined to tread. He would have come into conflict with the Jewish and Roman authorities before he completed his mission.

The Jews believed that the way to do God's will was to obey in every detail the Law of Moses which was contained in the first five books of the Old Testament. Jesus did not think that the Law was enough on its own. You had to obey it in the right way, in a spirit of loving kindness to all men, because above all God wanted men to love one another.

When Jesus healed on the Sabbath (3:1–6), he broke the Law since to heal is to work and work was forbidden on that day. But Jesus was making the point that it was more important to do good than blindly to obey a law. He did not say that the Law was wrong only that it could be over-ruled by a higher law – the law of love which was displayed in the act of healing.

Jesus no doubt knew that his teaching would eventually bring him into conflict with the religious authorities. It was not hard to predict that he would suffer, and Mark presents Jesus as explaining that he must suffer precisely because he was the Messiah (8:29–33).

Mark did not try to explain why this suffering was necessary to God's plan; it had simply to be accepted as a matter of faith. But he could look back to the Old Testament and see that God's messengers had repeatedly been rejected by the Israelites and suffered at their hands. In addition it was Mark's firm belief that everything that happened to Jesus was in accordance with God's will which had been revealed in the Old Testament (14:21, 49).

32

Mark shows Jesus asking whether he really has to suffer, and saying that he will accept it if it is God's will (14:36). It is easy to see how Mark's church could think of itself as being in the same position. They did not wish to suffer, but if it was God's will that they should then they would accept it, just as Jesus had.

Jesus was innocent of any crime yet he was executed, and now his innocent followers were also suffering. But if innocent suffering helped God's plan then it was not in vain. It was a suffering which lasted for only a limited time and the reward for bearing it was eternal bliss. So Mark's account of how Jesus bore his suffering encouraged his community and gave it strength to remain true to its faith.

(iii) Mark's suffering community

Although the Christians of Mark's church could see how Jesus suffered and understand it as the final victory over evil, it must still have been difficult for them to understand how it was possible for the Messiah to allow his followers to be persecuted by pagans.

If evil has been defeated, they must have asked, why are we suffering instead of being rewarded for faithfulness? Why has God's kingdom not come into being? Why are things still going on as before? One of Mark's aims was to provide reassurance in the face of these questions.

First, he made it clear that even Jesus felt that he had been abandoned. Jesus had cried out, 'My God, my God, why hast thou forsaken me?' (15:34). Mark's community too cried to God feeling abandoned in their suffering. Mark shows that Jesus had foreseen that both he and his followers would suffer. At 8:31 he taught that 'the Son of Man had to undergo great sufferings', and shortly after this he said, 'Anyone who wishes to be a follower of mine must leave self behind; he must take up his cross, and come with me' (8:34).

Mark's account of the good news told his community that its suffering had been foreseen by Jesus himself and, like the suffering of Jesus, was a part of God's plan.

Second, Mark pictured Jesus promising that the suffering would be only for a short time and the reward limitless. 'I tell you this: there are some of those standing here who will not taste death before they have seen the kingdom of God already come in power' (9:1). The belief that Jesus would return within the lifetime of people who had known him and establish God's kingdom was still widely held. If Jesus might return any day then suffering could be borne bravely.

The faith of the early church was continually tested to the limit. Christians must often have wondered whether they really did understand what was happening. Mark probably had such doubts in mind when he included the story of the healing of the blind man.

When Jesus first laid his hands on the man's eyes his sight was only partly restored. He could not see things clearly. 'I see men; they look like trees, but they are walking about.' When Jesus laid his hands on again the man saw everything clearly (8:22–26).

Mark and his church were like the blind man after the first laying on of hands. They knew what God's plan was; they knew that they would be rewarded eventually; they could see things dimly; but until Jesus came a second time they could not see clearly how their suffering fitted into God's plan. They had to have faith and be content with Jesus' promise that the kingdom of God would come, and that then they would understand everything.

Whenever we read Mark we must remember how he was influenced by the time and place in which he lived, and by the beliefs held by himself and his readers. He began his writing with several aims in mind. He wanted to explain the suffering of his church, the suffering of Jesus, and the secrecy about Jesus' Messiahship. But his overall aim was to try to understand the good news of Jesus and to explain it to his own community.

Questions for chapter 4

1. How did the time in which Mark lived influence what he wrote?

2. (a) What beliefs did Jews and Christians share in the first century AD?
   (b) Which readers did Mark have in mind when he wrote his gospel?

3. (a) Why was Jesus unable openly to claim the title 'Messiah'?
   (b) Why would Mark's church be interested in Jesus' insistence on secrecy?

II

The content of the gospel

Notes on the Political Background

Palestine was part of the Roman Empire during the first century AD.

Herod the Great (37 – 4 BC) ruled Palestine with the permission of Rome. On his death, the kingdom was divided up between his three sons,

Herod Archelaus ruled Judaea, Samaria and Idumaea, but was deposed in AD 6. From then on, Roman procurators were appointed. Pontius Pilate ruled from AD 26 – 36.

Herod Philip ruled Ituraea (4 BC – AD 34).

Herod Antipas ruled Galilee and Peraea (deposed by the Romans in AD 39).

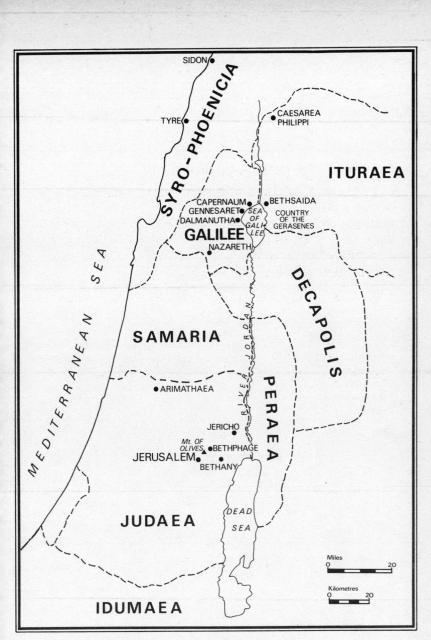

Palestine in the time of Christ

Place names referred to in Mark's gospel

Arimathaea, 15:43
Bethany, 11:1, 11, 12; 14:3
Bethphage, 11:1
Bethsaida, 6:45; 8:22
Caesarea Philippi, 8:27
Capernaum, 1:21; 2:1; 9:33
Dalmanutha, 8:10
Decapolis (or Ten Towns), 5:20; 7:31
Galilee, 1:14, 28, 39; 3:7, 6:21; 9:30; 14:28; 15:41; 16:7
Galilee, Sea of, 1:16, 7:31 (references to the 'sea' or 'lake'
    etc. not included)
Gennesaret, 6:53
Gerasenes, 5:1
Gethsemane, 14:32
Golgotha, 15:22
Idumaea, 3:8
Jericho, 10:46
Jerusalem, 1:5, 3:8, 22; 7:1; 10:33; 11:1, 11, 15, 27; 15:41
Jerusalem, road to, 10:32
Jordan, River, 1:5, 9
Jordan, beyond the (or Transjordan), 3:7, 10:1
Judaea, 1:5, 3:7, 10:1
Nazareth, 1:9 (also 'home town' 6:1) (references to 'Jesus
    of Nazareth' not included)
Olives, Mount of, 11:1, 13:3, 14:26
Sidon, 3:8, 7:24 (RSV), 31
Syro-Phoenicia, 7:26
Ten Towns, *see* Decapolis
Transjordan, *see* Jordan, beyond the
Tyre, 3:8; 7:24, 31

5.   The beginning of the gospel

Passages for study

1:1–15   Prologue
6:14–29   Death of John the Baptist

a. Mark links Jesus with past and future

(i) Mark works to a plan

To study Mark's gospel successfully you need to be something of a detective. Of course, a detective cannot do his
work unless he has something to go on, and so the first part
of this book has been designed to provide some clues. Our
task now is to examine the real evidence, that is the actual
words which Mark wrote.

  If we look at the first 15 verses of chapter 1 of Mark's
book it appears at first glance to be rather confused. He
covers a lot of ground in few words and seems to assume
that his readers will know what he is talking about. For
example, he says nothing of who John the Baptist was and
how he came to be in the wilderness. Neither does he give
us any background information about Jesus who, it seems,
suddenly turns up one day to be baptised. Presumably Mark
could have provided more detail if he had wished. No doubt
there were many appropriate stories in circulation at the
time. If, however, we examine these opening verses more
closely we can see that Mark had a plan which would not
allow for the sort of detailed information we might be interested in. He wanted to show his readers how in Jesus both
past and future were linked.

(ii) The link with the past

Mark starts his gospel in almost code-like fashion. He is
setting the scene for re-telling the story of Jesus, and he is
anxious to establish that Jesus is the Messiah for whom the

Jews were patiently waiting. In Jewish belief the Messiah would be heralded by a prophet, so in 1:2, 3 Mark quotes the prophecy and then in verses 4–8 casts John the Baptist in that very role. He even describes John's appearance which is, not by accident, strikingly similar to the appearance of the Old Testament prophet Elijah, thought by the Jews to be the most likely prophet to herald the Messiah. Mark is here trying to establish Jesus' pedigree in the minds of his readers. He is no upstart but one who has long been awaited.

(iii) The Messiah has come

The baptism of Jesus follows in verses 9–11. Mark wants his readers to know that God is present, so he describes in vivid language what happened as Jesus emerged from the water. The heavens opened, the Spirit descended on him like a dove and there was a voice from heaven which said, 'Thou art my Son, my Beloved; on thee my favour rests.' These words are similar to those found in the Old Testament at Psalm 2:7. This psalm is about the coronation of one of Israel's kings. When a person became king he was thought to be adopted by God and from then on would be treated as if he were God's son. As such he was God's representative on earth. In using these words, Mark is telling his readers that Jesus is God's new representative on earth. He is the Messiah whom the Jews have so long awaited.

(iv) Looking to the future

At the beginning of this chapter we said that Mark was working to a plan. We are now in a position to see this plan unfolding. He started off by linking Jesus with the past. The quotations from the Old Testament give John the Baptist and Jesus a place in Jewish history. Then came Jesus' baptism. This is really the beginning of the story which Mark is about to tell. Jesus has arrived on the scene and confirmation is received from heaven that he is the Messiah. We are no longer in the past but firmly in the present.

But what of the future? Mark himself is really in the future. Though he writes as if he were an eye-witness to the events, he is actually writing some 35 to 40 years after Jesus' death, basing his work on what he has been told by others about Jesus' life. Mark is in the period of the New Testament and at verse 15 he quotes a summary of the New Testament message, 'The time has come; the kingdom of God is upon you; repent, and believe the gospel.' The point in using this summary here is to show right at the beginning of the story that Jesus' message will go on into the future.

Mark's plan for the prologue is complete. He has firmly linked Jesus with the past and the future as the diagram below shows.

The stage is set. We have been introduced to the principal character. We have been made aware of who Jesus really is, and so we are in a position to appreciate more fully the action which is to follow.

OLD TESTAMENT →	JESUS	→ NEW TESTAMENT
Old Testament text which looks forward to the Messiah, *'Here is my herald.'*	The Old Testament voice which announces ← that Jesus is the Messiah, *'Thou art my Son.'*	The voice of the Christian preacher, ← *'The time has come.'*

Diagram showing how Jesus links the Old and New Testaments

b. Baptism

(i) A symbolic act

By the time Mark wrote, baptism was firmly established as the rite by which you became a Christian. Baptism itself was not uniquely Christian. The Jews baptised Gentile converts and, of course, John the Baptist himself was a Jew. Various forms of baptism were also used by people of other religions. In the Jewish and early Christian ceremony, people who wished to become full members of either religion were completely immersed in water. Through this symbolic act the converts were thought to be made clean of their past wrong-doings and their old style of life, and so given a fresh start.

(ii) Mark's understanding of baptism

Mark saw an even deeper significance in baptism. For him it was closely associated with the death and resurrection of Jesus. It was perhaps his situation which made him think about the close connection between the two.

He was writing from Rome, the centre of persecution of Christians at the time. As we have seen, to become a Christian in those days meant putting yourself at terrible risk. Arrest, persecution and death for your faith were distinct possibilities which you had to learn to live with. Mark knew that the suffering of his community was not unique. Jesus too had suffered terribly at the hands of his oppressors, dying an agonising death on the cross. But the Christian belief and hope then, as now, was that death was not the end – Jesus had risen from the dead.

Mark believed that those faithful Christians who had suffered death for their faith would also be given new life, and the symbolic way of expressing this was by baptism. When a convert was baptised he was not simply given a fresh start, he died to an old way of life and was given new life as a disciple of Jesus. Baptism was the way in which you started your Christian life. By being fully immersed in water you were forcefully reminded that death was a real possibility, but of equal importance, you were assured of the resurrection. Mark chooses to start his gospel in the way he ends it, because for Mark baptism is a symbol of the death and resurrection of Jesus.

It is also important to notice that Mark places the temptation immediately after Jesus' baptism. He is driving home the consequences of becoming a Christian. It is no soft option. Mark does not say that Jesus was victorious over Satan but is perhaps implying that the fight against evil begins as soon as you start your Christian life.

c. John the Baptist

(i) His message

We learn more of John the Baptist from Matthew and Luke than we do from Mark. They both give detailed information about his teaching, and Luke even tells us of the events surrounding his birth. However, as we shall see later, Mark does give us a detailed account of how John came to die.

It has already been pointed out that John's appearance was strikingly similar to that of the Jewish prophet Elijah. John works in the wilderness and this too is significant. Where else could it be, for the Old Testament prophecy, must be fulfilled, 'A voice crying aloud in the wilderness' (1:3).

John, then, stands in the tradition of the Old Testament, but he points directly to Jesus ('After me comes one who is mightier than I'). For Mark, John is the *forerunner*, preparing the people for the arrival of the Messiah, standing in the wilderness like a signpost. His message was that the people should 'repent'. That did not mean simply saying sorry but involved a complete change of heart, and baptism signified this turning away from an old way of life to one that was completely new. In baptising, John shows himself to be different from the prophets and it is significant that the people he baptises are Jews. He warns them that his water baptism is but a preparation for baptism with the Holy Spirit which the Messiah will bring, yet when Jesus arrives on the scene he also undergoes baptism at the hands of John.

Two other references in Mark tell us that John had disciples (2:18), and also that he was generally regarded by the people as a prophet (11:32). Some scholars today believe that John may have been connected in some way with the Essenes who lived a monastic life near the shores of the Dead Sea.

(ii) His death

Before Jesus actually commenced his ministry, Mark tells us that John was arrested. Later on in his gospel (6:14–29), he informs us of the events surrounding John's death. Apparently John had fallen foul of Herod Antipas (tetrarch or ruler of Galilee) by speaking out against his marriage.

Herod had divorced his first wife and then married Herodias, his brother's wife. There were Old Testament rules which said this was wrong and John had told Herod so. Mark tells us that it was out of spite that Herodias persuaded her daughter to ask Herod to have John beheaded. Reluctantly Herod agreed because he had made a promise to give the girl whatever she asked, but Mark would have us believe that deep down Herod wanted John kept alive, 'for Herod went in awe of John, knowing him to be a good and holy man' (6:20). John's message puzzled Herod yet, despite this, verse 20 tells us that Herod liked to listen to him.

The Jewish historian Josephus, writing probably some sixty years after John's death, gives a different reason for the Baptist's execution. He says that Herod feared that John might be a dangerous nationalist revolutionary, and for that reason he had him killed.

d. Additional notes

1. The prophecy Mark quotes in 1:2, 3 is in fact a combination of Malachi 3:1 and Isaiah 40:3 and not just Isaiah as Mark says. It may have been that Mark was quoting from memory not troubling to check his sources or that the two texts were already combined in some collection of prophecies Mark was using.

2. For a description of Elijah look up 2 Kings 1:8 and compare this with Mark's description of John the Baptist in 1:6. According to Malachi 4:5–6, Elijah would return before God's final intervention.

3. We have already noted the close connection Mark makes between baptism and temptation. The dedication shown in baptism is put to the test when evil is encountered. This theme is further developed in the gospel and will receive more detailed comment in chapters 7 and 9.

Questions for chapter 5

1. What did John the Baptist wear and what did he eat?

2. What was John the Baptist's message and what was the purpose of his work?

3. Describe how John the Baptist came to die.

4. Describe what happened at Jesus' baptism.

5. What is the significance of baptism in Mark's gospel?

6. How does Mark explain to his readers who Jesus really is?

6. The disciples

a. How Mark portrays the disciples

(i) The call of the disciples

A disciple is someone who is a pupil and follower of a teacher. Jesus followed the custom of the rabbis of his time and gathered round him a group of disciples to whom he passed on his teaching. This group seems to have been quite large and from it he chose twelve close companions (3:13 – 19a).

The most striking thing about the disciples chosen by Jesus is how ordinary they were. Those we know about were fishermen, a tax-collector and a Zealot. (The Zealots were Jewish nationalists who wanted to be free of Roman rule.) There were no representatives of religion among the disciples as far as we can tell: no priests, doctors of the Law or Pharisees. They were laymen, the same everyday people as the members of Mark's church, and their trades showed that Christianity was not to be a religion of experts.

When Mark introduces the disciples he presents them going about their daily business. Simon (Peter) and his brother Andrew were working with a casting net on the Sea of Galilee, and James and his brother John were overhauling their nets (1:16–20). They are ordinary people with ordinary lives and possessions.

Then the extraordinary happens. Jesus comes along and calls them to follow him, and they do so immediately leaving everything behind.

The same thing happens when Jesus calls Levi from the custom-house (2:13–14). In Jewish eyes he is a sinner: he probably mixes with Romans, he collects their taxes and does not keep the Law. But it makes no difference, he is still called to follow Jesus.

Mark makes use of these scenes to teach how men should respond when called to follow Jesus: they must act immediately. To become a Christian is to begin a new life, and we may be called on to abandon job and possessions. The true disciple must be prepared to leave everything for Jesus without hesitation.

(ii) The cost of following Jesus

The early Christians discovered that when they became followers of Jesus not all members of their families would leave their pagan or Jewish ways and join them. Families were torn apart. Then the new Christians needed to know which was more important – family or Jesus? Mark gave the answer in the case of James and John, 'leaving their father Zebedee in the boat with the hired men, they went off to follow him (Jesus)' (1:20). Mark also puts the words 'we here have left everything to become your followers' into Peter's mouth, and Jesus responds by promising a rich reward to those who give up their families for his sake (10:28–30).

Mark gives still further reassurance to those cut off from their families. Jesus himself rejects his family when they do not understand what he is doing. He says, 'Whoever does the will of God is my brother, my sister, my mother' (3:21, 31–35).

The call of the disciples taught Christians that all were called equally, that they had to respond immediately, and that they had to be prepared to give up everything; but also that they would not be alone because they would be members of one new family which included Jesus.

b. The Twelve*

Jesus had many disciples but three seem to have been especially close to him. They are Simon, to whom Jesus gave the name Peter (3:16), James and his brother John. These three witness Jesus' transfiguration and are chosen to be with him when he prays before his arrest at Gethsemane. In spite of failing Jesus several times, Peter is presented by Mark as the leader of the disciples, and in the Acts of the

* Mark calls the disciples 'Apostles' on only one occasion in his gospel. This is when he describes the return of the Twelve from a mission on which Jesus had sent them (6:7–13, 30). Appropriately enough, the word apostle means 'one who is *sent*'.

Apostles (1:15) he still appears to hold this position after the death of Jesus.

This inner group of three was part of a larger group, the Twelve, who were selected by Jesus 'as his companions' (3:14). At the time of Jesus numbers had meanings attached to them beyond their normal use for reckoning. So, if Jesus chose twelve companions and if Mark goes to the trouble of emphasising this by listing their names, we must ask what this number signified.

In the Old Testament there were twelve tribes of Israel who were chosen by God to be his special people providing that they obeyed the laws which he gave to Moses (Exod. 19:5). When Jesus chooses twelve disciples he seems to be saying that these men are to be the nucleus of a new people of God. Since Israel has failed to keep the laws in the spirit in which God intended, a new people and new teachings are needed.

The Twelve are shown by Mark to be the first members of a new covenant or agreement with God (14:22–25). He saw them as the founders of the Christian church, for just as the people of Israel were descended from the twelve sons of Jacob, so the members of his church were, in a parallel way, the successors of the Twelve.

All that you had to do to be a member of this new covenant was to join the church and to live and believe as Jesus taught. In other words – be his disciple.

c. The church imitates the disciples

Christians of Mark's generation repeated words and imitated actions which they believed had originally been spoken and performed by Jesus and the disciples. The same is true of Christians today.

The most important words spoken by any of the disciples are those of Peter when the Twelve are with Jesus on the road to Caesarea Philippi (8:27–29). Jesus asks the disciples who men were saying that he was. They reply that some say he is John the Baptist, others Elijah, and others one of the prophets.

Then Jesus asks the vital question, *'Who do you say I am?'* Peter answers for the disciples and for every succeeding generation of Christians, *'You are the Messiah'*. This is the Christian confession of faith, and it is made first of all by the foremost of the disciples. Everyone who becomes a Christian follows Peter in confessing that Jesus is none other than the Messiah.

Mark's accounts of the actions of the Twelve not only show how they behaved but also how the members of his church behaved.

The Communion was the most important service in Mark's church, as it is in most churches today. It is a re-enactment of the Last Supper (14:22–25). During it the actions of Jesus are imitated by the person conducting the service, and the congregation imitates the disciples who received the bread and wine from Jesus himself. When Mark describes the Last Supper, he makes use of the oral tradition of the church and of his knowledge of what is said and done at the Communion service in order to picture the original event.

There is probably the same mixing of oral tradition and his own church's experience when he describes the mission of the Twelve (6:7–13).

The oral tradition preserved a memory of Jesus sending disciples out to teach and heal. When Mark describes the event he turns to the experience of his own church to provide the details of how the disciples were equipped. Since he and his fellow Christians imitated the Twelve it was natural for him to think that the missionaries they had come into contact with were identical to those originally despatched by Jesus.

But conditions varied widely in different parts of the Roman Empire and how the missionaries dressed and what they carried varied according to local conditions. So Mark's description of the Twelve being sent on a mission reflects the conditions he was familiar with in his part of the world.

The early Christians tried to imitate the disciples and believed that their customs came directly from them. However, Mark's accounts of the disciples often tell as much about his church and its practices as about the disciples themselves.

d. The disciples' failures and temptations

(i) The failings of ordinary Christians

The disciples called by Jesus had the faults of ordinary men and in Mark we see these faults more clearly than in any other gospel. We suggested in chapter 3 that one reason for this might be that Peter supplied Mark with information and that he gave an honest account of the disciples' failings.

Another reason for the poor picture of the disciples in Mark is that he was twenty years closer to the events he describes than the writers of the other synoptic gospels. By the time Matthew and Luke wrote, none of the disciples would have been still living and when the church looked back to its founders it tended to idealise them: to make them larger than life and more perfect than perhaps they were. We all do this with people we regard as heroes. You can see an example of this polishing of the disciples' image if you look up Mark 4:38 and Luke 8:24. Luke uses Mark's account of the Stilling of the Storm but where Mark has the disciples ask Jesus accusingly, 'Do you not care?' Luke leaves out the question. It seems that by Luke's time the idea that the disciples would suggest Jesus might not care what happened to them was too disrespectful to the memory of such *extraordinary* men to be included.

Mark does not record the failings of the disciples in order to present an accurate historical picture of them. In everything he writes he aims to help the Christians he knows and he makes use of his knowledge with this end in mind.

We have said that the disciples were the founder members of the church and that the church imitated the actions of the disciples and saw itself reflected in them. When Mark shows the disciples lacking faith (4:40) or understanding (8:14–21), or being afraid (9:6), or arguing about who was the greatest (9:33–37), the members of his church could see themselves struggling with the same diffulties as had troubled the disciples themselves.

(ii) Facing difficulties and temptations

The teachings of Jesus were not easy to live by; there were constant temptations to lead you astray. For Mark all temptation came from one source – Satan. The temptation of Jesus started immediately after his baptism and opposition to him continued until his death. In Mark's time the opposition was directed against the church. Everyone who was a Christian was a target for Satan.

The temptation to avoid the difficult path Jesus had mapped out for himself and his followers could seize anyone. Even Peter wanted Jesus to avoid the suffering which obedience to God would bring. Jesus answered Peter with the words, 'Away with you Satan' (8:33). The lesson for the church was clear: whenever temptation arises it is the work of Satan and must be rejected.

The disciples receive warnings from Jesus that to follow him means being prepared to sacrifice themselves. 'Anyone who wishes to be a follower of mine must leave self behind; he must take up his cross, and come with me' (8:34). It meant being prepared to suffer.

When James and John ask to have places of honour in the kingdom of God, Jesus prophesies that they will drink the cup he drinks and be baptised with his baptism (10:35–40). The cup stands for suffering and to be baptised like Jesus means to die with him. Jesus' warnings to the disciples apply to the church: to follow him is to risk everything for the kingdom of God.

In spite of these warnings people became Christians, but when the time of testing came they sometimes failed. Did this mean that Jesus would disown them? Mark records an incident which provides an answer.

After the Last Supper Jesus and the Twelve were on the Mount of Olives. Jesus told them that they would all fall from their faith. They all denied it, especially Peter (14:26–31). Yet when Jesus was arrested they all fled and Peter denied him three times. But even after this Jesus did not abandon them. After the crucifixion when the women went to Jesus' tomb and learned that he was risen they were given a message for Peter and the disciples (16:1–8).

The message this incident carried for the church was that if Jesus chose such fallible men to be his disciples, then there was hope and forgiveness for the ordinary weak men and women who made up the Christian church. The disciples in Mark's gospel gave encouragement to the church which came after them.

(iii) The traitor

There is one exception to Mark's message of hope – Judas Iscariot. He is the example of the disciple who turns and betrays his master. He is completely in the power of Satan, but even so he cannot help but play his part in fulfilling God's plan.

Jesus says, 'The Son of Man is going the way appointed for him in the scriptures; but alas for that man by whom the Son of Man is betrayed! It would be better for that man if he had never been born' (14:21). This, according to Mark, is Jesus' only comment on Judas. The message is final: there is no hope for you if you are as hopelessly in Satan's power as is Judas.

e. The Twelve   3:13–19

Simon Peter

Mark puts the call of Simon the fisherman and his brother, Andrew, before that of any other disciple (1:16–18). He also puts Simon at the head of the list of the Twelve. He appears as their spokesman throughout the gospel and after the death of Jesus he keeps this position (see Acts 1:15). It is he who makes the great confession of faith that Jesus is the Messiah (8:29). Jesus gives him the name Peter on his appointment to the Twelve and from this point Mark uses that name instead of Simon. Peter means 'rock' but Mark does not explain why his name was changed. Matthew (16:18–19) expands this event by explaining that Peter was to be the rock on which Jesus would build his church. After Jesus' arrest Peter does not display a very rock-like character but denies him three times (14:66–72). In Mark's gospel the final message from Jesus is addressed to Peter and the disciples. Peter is thought to have died in Rome during the persecution of Christians by Nero in about AD 64, and he may have been one of Mark's sources.

James the son of Zebedee

He and his brother John were fishermen. They left their boat and father when called by Jesus (1:19–20). He is one of the three disciples closest to Jesus but he is always referred to together with his brother such as when they ask to sit in state with Jesus (10:35–40). He and John were given the title 'Boanerges' which Mark says means 'Sons of Thunder'. It is not clear why this name was given. Luke says that they wanted to call down fire from heaven on a village (Luke 9:51–56). To call someone 'son of something' meant that the person had that particular characteristic, so perhaps the brothers were in some way thunderous.

John the son of Zebedee
(See the note about his brother James.) He is usually linked with his brother. He is the disciple who tells Jesus that they tried to stop a man driving out devils in Jesus' name (9:38–41).

Andrew
He was a fisherman like his brother Simon Peter, but in comparison he occupies a position of minor importance. He was present when Simon Peter's mother-in-law was healed (1:29–31), and on the Mount of Olives with Jesus and his three closest disciples (13:3). In John's gospel Andrew is said to be a disciple of John the Baptist (John 1:35–42).

Philip
Although his name appears in fifth place in Mark's list of the Twelve it does not occur again in his gospel. In John's gospel Philip is said to come from Bethsaida (John 1:44).

Bartholomew
Apart from being mentioned in the list of the Twelve nothing is known about him.

Matthew
Nothing certain is known about him. In Matthew's gospel (not written by this Matthew) Matthew the apostle is called the 'tax-gatherer'. Mark describes the call of the man in the custom-house who is named Levi (2:14). In the account of this in Matthew's gospel (Matt. 9:9) the name Levi is changed to Matthew. This has led some people to suggest that Matthew and Levi are the same person. Since Mark does not identify the one with the other we should be cautious about doing so.

Thomas
The only place where Thomas's name appears in Mark's gospel is in the list of the Twelve. In John's gospel Thomas is called 'Didymus', meaning 'the twin', but nothing is

known about his twin. In the same gospel Thomas is the apostle who refused to believe that Jesus had risen until he could see the marks of the nails and put his hand into his side (John 20:24–25); hence our expression 'doubting Thomas'.

James the son of Alphaeus
Apart from this mention in the list of the Twelve we know nothing about him. Since Levi is also called 'son of Alphaeus' (2:14) the suggestion has been made that James and Levi were either two names for one person or brothers. Mark mentions a 'James the younger' (15:40) and it has been suggested that he is the same James as in the list of the Twelve. There is, however, no firm evidence to support any of these suggestions.

Thaddeus
He does not appear in the list of the Twelve given by Luke (Luke 6:14–16), and in some ancient manuscripts of Mark the name is given as Lebbaeus. Nothing is known about him.

Simon the Zealot
The New English Bible says 'Simon, a member of the Zealot party', which is not an accurate translation of Mark. In the original, Mark uses the word 'Cananean' which simply means 'zealous'. It is thought though that Mark intended to indicate that Simon belonged to a group which later became known as the Zealot party. If he were indeed a member of this group, Jesus was clearly running a risk in choosing someone involved in politics to be one of his companions. The Zealots were Jewish nationalists whose aim was to drive the Romans out of Palestine. They were in the forefront of the rebellion against the Romans in AD 66–70. Apart from being listed as one of the Twelve there is no other mention of him in the gospel.

Judas Iscariot
The man who betrayed Jesus appears last on the list. The name 'Iscariot' probably means 'the man from Kerioth', a town in southern Judaea. This would mean that he was most likely the only non-Galilean of the Twelve. He is only mentioned in Mark in the list of the Twelve and on the occasion when he betrays Jesus (14:10–11, 43–45). Mark gives no

56

reason for the betrayal. The chief priests offer him money, but according to Mark this is after he has offered to betray Jesus not before. Matthew says that the sum was thirty pieces of silver (Matt. 26:15). He also says that Judas hanged himself (Matt. 27:5). In the Acts of the Apostles we are simply told that after buying a plot of land Judas fell down dead (Acts 1:18). In Matthew and John's accounts of the Last Supper, Jesus is shown as knowing that Judas will betray him (Matt. 26:25; John 13:26–28).

f. References to the disciples

1:16–20
2:13–14
3:13–19
4:40–41
5:37
6:7–13, 30–32, 37, 51–52
7:18
8:14–21, 27–30
9:2, 6, 14–29, 30–37
10:13, 35–40, 41–45
11:1–11, 14, 20–21
13:1–4
14:17–21, 26–31, 32–42, 43–50, 66–72

Questions for chapter 6

1. (a) Describe the call of (i) James and John, (ii) Levi.
   (b) What did their response to Jesus' call teach about discipleship?

2. (a) Who are the three disciples closest to Jesus?
   (b) Describe an event which occurs when they are with Jesus.

3. (a) Describe the appointment of the Twelve.
   (b) Why did Jesus choose *twelve* companions?

4. (a) Describe two or three occasions on which the disciples displayed human weakness.

(b) Explain how Mark's account of these incidents could have helped his church.

5. 'The disciples were the nucleus of the church'. What do you understand by this statement?

7. The conflict with authority

a. The one enemy, Satan

According to Mark, 'Jesus came into Galilee proclaiming the Gospel of God: "The time has come; the kingdom of God is upon you; repent and believe the gospel" ' (1:14–15). Jesus had come to fulfil the prophecies of the Old Testament. He came to proclaim the good news, and to call people to change their way of life so that they could enjoy the kingdom of God which was at hand.

This was the event that the Jews had been anticipating for centuries. Why, then, should there be conflict? Why was Jesus put to death instead of being welcomed as the Messiah?

To understand how Mark answered these questions we must remind ourselves of the beliefs that Christians of his time held about the universe. They believed that God had originally created a perfect world, but during the time since then the forces of evil had succeeded in gaining control of much of creation. God planned to bring his creation to a perfect conclusion but before that could happen evil had to be defeated. Jesus was the one sent by God to fight the final battle against evil.

As Mark saw things, it was inevitable that as soon as the powers of evil realised who Jesus was he should be involved in conflict. To emphasise the point Mark showed Jesus' ministry beginning with a contest with Satan. Immediately after his baptism by John, Jesus went away into the wilderness for forty days to be 'tempted by Satan' (1:12–13).

From this moment Jesus is in conflict with evil almost constantly. Evil comes in many disguises, but anyone who is against him is against the Holy Spirit which entered him at his baptism. The Holy Spirit is God's power in the world, and anyone opposing it is opposing God and serving evil. The Pharisees, Sadducees, doctors of the law, Herodians, chief priests, Pilate, Judas Iscariot, at times even the other

59

disciples serve evil when they oppose Jesus. But evil does not take human form alone. In his miracles too, Jesus is in conflict with the workings of evil.

We can see how Mark saw the two sides in the battle if we list the qualities of each.

Jesus	Satan
life	death
health	sickness
order	chaos
love	hate
good	evil

Everything Jesus stood for was opposed by the evil in the world represented by Satan. For Mark this background of belief set the scene against which Jesus went about his work. Jesus had come to defeat evil, therefore conflict with the forces of evil was inevitable.

b. Christians and conflict

The beliefs which the early Christians held about the battle between good and evil provided them with an explanation for their own situation.

During Jesus' lifetime there had been opposition to him and his followers, first by the religious authorities and then by the Romans. Since his death this opposition had been directed against the church which was continuing his work.

Mark wrote for Christians living in a hostile world. It appeared to them to be an evil age in which the pagan rulers of the world served the powers of evil.

The same situation existed between the church and its enemies as had existed between Jesus and his enemies. Just as Jesus had been filled with the Holy Spirit and anyone against him was against God, so now in Mark's time the church was filled with the Holy Spirit and to be against the church was to be against God. In both cases the opponents of God's representatives on earth served Satan.

To continue to hold fast to one's faith in dangerous circumstances was difficult and Mark probably had in mind the need to encourage his fellow Christians when he included Jesus' warning about the fate awaiting his disciples. The warning reflects the events of Jesus' own life and of the life of the church after his death. 'You will be handed over to the courts. You will be flogged in synagogues. You will be summoned to appear before governors and kings on my account to testify in their presence.' But the church had to press on with its mission in spite of the opposition, because before Jesus returned on the day of judgment 'the Gospel must be proclaimed to all nations' (13:9–10).

In these circumstances Mark's interest in conflict is easy to understand. The Christians he wrote for saw themselves living in the centre of a cosmic battle between good and evil. Their victory was assured, but they were only human and needed encouragement to fight on. They drew strength from the accounts of Jesus' own struggle with evil and from seeing how he had triumphed over the very same enemy which now, as he had prophesied, confronted them.

c. How Mark charts the opposition to Jesus

(i) The early opposition to Jesus   2:1–3:6

In Mark's gospel, conflict arises whenever Jesus comes into contact with the religious authorities. After the introduction to the gospel which states who Jesus is and a short section which outlines his teaching and the signs he will perform, Mark presents the opposition.

We must remember that Mark's portrait of the Jewish authorities is coloured by his view of them. He believed that they were evil and responsible for the death of Jesus. So he thinks he is right to paint them in the worst light possible.

The first group to come into conflict with Jesus are the doctors of the law or scribes (2:1–12). A paralysed man is brought to Jesus, but instead of simply healing him Jesus tells him, 'My son, your sins are forgiven.' The lawyers regard this as blasphemy as only God can forgive sins. In order to show that he has the right to offer forgiveness, Jesus then heals the man. To forgive sins and to heal are both ways of freeing someone from the consequences of evil.

This miracle story introduces the first hint of human opposition to Jesus. It links up with his trial which is the final act of opposition by the religious authorities. In both cases the charge against Jesus is blasphemy. The lawyers, like the Sanhedrin, are unable to recognise Jesus' true identity. If they could then they would know that he could not blaspheme because he is guided by the Holy Spirit.

In the next section the Pharisees join the opposition (2:15–3:6). First they are shocked that Jesus eats with sinners, then they object to the disciples and Jesus ignoring the rules about Sabbath behaviour.

In these cases the opposition centres on the observance of religious laws. The Pharisees had developed a multitude of minute rules to cover every occasion and insisted that it was necessary to obey every one in order to be a good Jew.

When Jesus eats with sinners he is making himself religiously impure, and Mark implies that the Pharisees regard being pure more important than trying to save sinners from their evil ways. It is the same story when Jesus heals on the Sabbath. The Pharisees think that it is more important to obey the Sabbath laws than to help a man with a withered arm.

Jesus cuts through all their petty rules, and by his actions shows that people are more important and that God did not intend the Sabbath commandment to mean that men should suffer longer than necessary. This is summed up in the saying of Jesus, 'The Sabbath was made for the sake of man and not man for the Sabbath' (2:27). The Pharisees are blind to the spirit of the law and to their own failings. Really it is they who need a doctor as much as the tax-gatherers.

This section of the gospel ends with Mark saying that the Pharisees and the partisans of Herod began plotting together against Jesus. This is the third hostile group to be identified. Mark only mentions the Herodians three times and in each case they are linked with the Pharisees. They were supporters of the dynasty of the Herods and strongly nationalistic.

This meant that both religious and political Jews were against Jesus: all the representatives of God's chosen people rejected the Messiah he had sent to them. It was only the ordinary people who flocked to him.

(ii) Jesus attacks the opposition

Mark does not present Jesus as a meek and mild Messiah. Although his life would end in suffering because of his obedience to God's will, this did not mean that he should remain silent when he met evil. His task was to defeat it.

Jesus condemns the Pharisees and lawyers as hypocrites because they only pay lip-service to God: their hearts are not in their worship. He also accuses them of neglecting the commandments of God (7:6–8).

Jesus not only condemns but also takes direct action to get rid of evil. When he reaches Jerusalem he enters the temple, the very centre of the religion and the centre of opposition to him. He upsets the money-changers' tables and accuses them of having allowed the temple to become a robbers' cave instead of a house of prayer. His enemies were now plotting to kill him, but were unable to because of the crowds which followed him (11:15–19; 12:12).

Although Jesus realises that his days are numbered he does not hide but preaches daily and mocks the plotters. He makes fun of the doctors of the law parading up and down in their long robes, and of their desire for the important seats in the synagogues, and he points out how they swindle helpless widows (12:38–40).

In Mark's gospel Jesus' final words to those opposed to him are spoken at his trial before the Sanhedrin. When the High Priest asks, 'Are you the Messiah, the Son of the Blessed One?' Jesus replies, 'I am; and you will see the Son of Man seated at the right hand of God and coming with the clouds of heaven' (14:61b–62).

This reply condemns his opponents for all time. Jesus' words meant that at the Day of Judgment he would return and those who had opposed him, and were at that moment trying him, would be sure to perish.

(iii) Jerusalem, the centre of opposition

Mark builds up a picture of increasing opposition as his gospel proceeds. When the doctors of the law are mentioned at 3:22 he says that they 'had come down from Jerusalem'. This was the centre of Judaism and Mark wants us to understand that the reaction of these lawyers is the reaction of official Judaism to Jesus.

They fail to see who Jesus really is and accuse him of being possessed by Beelzebub, a prince of demons. By this slander of the Holy Spirit whose power is in Jesus, they condemn themselves. Mark drives home the point that the lawyers are totally in the power of evil and beyond saving by following their accusation with Jesus' saying, 'No sin, no slander, is beyond forgiveness for men; but whoever slanders the Holy Spirit can never be forgiven; he is guilty of eternal sin' (3:28–29).

Jerusalem is the place where the Messiah must be proclaimed King by God's chosen people. But there is little chance of the religious leaders hailing Jesus, and he several times foretells what will happen to him.

At the point in the gospel where Jesus turns towards Jerusalem, Mark pictures him prophesying to his disciples how the conflict will end, 'the Son of Man will be given up to the chief priests and the doctors of the law; they will condemn him to death and hand him over to the foreign power' (10:33). This prophetic summary introduces two more groups who oppose Jesus: the chief priests and the Roman authorities.

Once in Jerusalem, all those opposing him set about trying to trap him into committing blasphemy or speaking against the Romans. Either offence would give them the excuse they needed to arrest him.

Mark lists Jesus' opponents and their questions in succession. 11:27–33: the chief priests, lawyers and elders (the three groups which made up the Sanhedrin) ask about authority. 12:13–17: the Pharisees and men of Herod's party ask about paying taxes to the Roman Emperor. 12:18–25: the Sadducees ask about the resurrection of the dead. They all fail to trap him and it is only his betrayal by Judas that eventually places him in their power.

The climax of the conflict is the trial and crucifixion. There is no evidence to convict Jesus but, according to Mark, when the High Priest asks Jesus, 'Are you the Messiah?' (14:61) he admits that he is and is found guilty of blasphemy. The High Priest and Council condemn themselves by their judgment. They cannot see that Jesus is the Messiah and that what he says is not blasphemy but the truth.

The importance for Mark of this repeated theme of the blindness of the Jews was that it meant that they were no longer fit to remain the chosen people of God, and this role passed to the new people of God: the church to which Mark belonged.

64

The day following the trial Jesus is taken by the chief priests before Pilate, the Roman governor, and is accused of claiming to be the King of the Jews. Again it is the blindness of the Jewish authorities which prevents them seeing that as the Messiah he really is King of the Jews.

The trial, as Mark describes it, does not follow Roman rules for a court of law. But the point he wants to make is that Jesus is rejected by the political rulers of the world as well as the religious – just as his church will be.

When Jesus is crucified evil seems to have won, but not even death, Satan's most powerful weapon, can defeat him. He rises from the dead and shows that, when the time comes, evil will be conquered.

In spite of the almost endless opposition to Jesus, the message for Christians in Mark's gospel is one of hope. The hostility which Jesus met, and which is still directed against the church, cannot finally win. But until Jesus returns on the Day of Judgment and destroys evil, conflict will continue, because those serving evil are blind both to the truth about Jesus and to the hopelessness of their position.

d. The Jewish authorities

Doctors of the Law or lawyers or scribes

The Greek word used by Mark meant 'scribe', a person who was simply a clerk, but the Jewish scribes were more than this. They not only made copies of the scrolls of the Law, and so became expert in it, but they learned by heart many past legal cases in which the Law had been used to settle disputes. When new disputes arose they would quote previous judgments and the matter would be settled in accordance with tradition. (There is a reference to tradition at 7:3.) The translation of 'scribe' as 'doctor of the law' in the New English Bible is intended to indicate that they were scholarly experts in the Law.

They often had their own groups of disciples to whom they passed on their knowledge and in many ways Jesus and his disciples resembled them. The surprise Jesus caused at Capernaum was because he spoke with authority, not like the doctors of the law who quoted tradition rather than giving original teachings (1:27).

The lawyers were respected members of their community and were addressed as rabbi, teacher. Being a lawyer was not a paid profession and unless they were wealthy they worked for their living. The majority of them lived in Jerusalem and Mark mentions that some of them came down to listen to Jesus (3:22).

They were not a religious party themselves and many of them belonged to the Pharisees' party while others were Sadducees. They were represented in the Sanhedrin and Mark says that the plan to hand Jesus over to Pilate was made between the chief priests, elders and lawyers (15:1). Not all lawyers seem to have opposed Jesus and Mark records an incident when Jesus tells one that he is not far from the kingdom of God (12:28–34).

Pharisees

The name 'Pharisees' seems to have meant 'the separated ones'. It indicated that they wished to remain apart from those who did not observe the Law (e.g. tax-gatherers), from pagan customs (those of the Romans), and from religious impurity (anyone ritually unclean, lepers etc.).

They were extremely devout and attempted to keep the Law of Moses in every detail. They also preserved oral traditions which they treated as being of equal importance to the Law. They were probably successors to the Maccabees and Hasmonaeans, Jewish dynasties which had resisted the spread of Greek ideas in the second century BC.

Unlike the Sadducees, the Pharisees believed that after death there would, at some time in the future, be resurrection to a new life for law-abiding Jews. They also believed that angels and spirits brought men messages from God. Neither of these beliefs is precisely stated in the books of Moses but they were developed later as a result of persecution. Jesus' differences with them arose mainly because of their insistence on sticking to every detail of the Law regardless of the consequences (see 3:1–6).

Although some Pharisees were priests most were laymen who banded together to live by the Law. Modern Judaism is derived from the Pharisees because unlike the Sadducees they were not attached to the temple and survived its destruction in AD 70.

Sadducees

The Sadducees were the aristocratic party. Their name might have meant 'the righteous ones', or, since many of them were priests, may have been connected with the name Zadok, a priest who lived at the time of David and Solomon.

The High Priest was appointed from among their number, and they controlled the Sanhedrin and the temple. They were only able to exercise this power because they co-operated with the Romans. Ever since the party had arisen during the second century BC the Sadducees had favoured a policy of compromise with pagan ideas. The ruling dynasty of that time, the Maccabees, had opposed pagan customs and this policy was continued in Jesus' time by the Pharisees.

The Pharisees and the Zealots were not popular with the Sadducees because both criticised them; the former for not being strict Jews, the latter for not resisting the Romans. The Sadducees possibly saw Jesus as a source of trouble in their dealings with the Romans and as a threat to their authority.

The Sadducees based their beliefs firmly on the books of Moses with none of the Pharisees' additions such as resurrection, angels and spirits. They believed in a shadowy afterlife for all men in Sheol. This was why they were shown by Mark to ask a question about resurrection when trying to trap Jesus (12:18–25).

When the temple was destroyed in AD 70 the Sanhedrin ceased to exist and the Sadducees' party came to an end.

Herodians

The partisans of Herod or men of Herod's party were supporters of the dynasty of the Herods. They were nationalists who wished to be rid of the Romans but, like the Sadducees, were forced to compromise with their conquerors in order to keep their power. The Romans allowed the Herods to rule various parts of Palestine and although they presented themselves as Jewish kings they were happy to adopt pagan customs. If, as Mark says, the Herodians and the Pharisees plotted together against Jesus it must have been because the Herodians, like the Sadducees, thought him a political trouble-maker. They would not have been worried about his criticisms of the Pharisees nor theirs of him.

John the Baptist was beheaded by Herod Antipas, the son of Herod the Great who is the King Herod in the story of the astrologers and the massacre of the children (Mark 6:14–29; Matt. 2). Mark mentions the partisans of Herod only three times, 3:6; 8:15; 12:13.

Priests

Priests were in charge of the temple in Jerusalem and it was their job to offer prayers and sacrifices on their own behalf and that of the whole people in accordance with the Law of Moses. They conducted the daily offerings and the large annual festivals such as the Passover to which thousands of people came. The leper healed by Jesus was told to show himself to the priest and make the offering laid down by Moses (1:44).

The High Priest was the only person allowed to enter the Holy of Holies, the most sacred place in the temple, and then only once a year on the Day of Atonement. He held the position of president of the Sanhedrin and it was his and the council's duty to see that the religious and national laws were obeyed. When Jesus is brought before the council or court it appears to be on religious grounds (14:55–64).

The chief priests referred to by Mark were probably those priests from important families who were members of the Sanhedrin. There was no class of priests with that precise title.

Elders

When Mark refers to the elders he means one of the three classes of people who made up the Sanhedrin. (The others were priests and lawyers.) They were laymen who were respected by their communities. Mark mentions them only three times, 8:31; 11:27; 15:1.

The Sanhedrin

The word 'Sanhedrin' means 'council'. It was the Jewish ruling council and was also a court which enforced Jewish laws. It had a force of temple police at its service and the right to arrest people. Three classes of people belonged to the Sanhedrin – priests, doctors of the law and elders. Since they also belonged to the Pharisees' and Sadducees' parties and many came from aristocratic families, the Sanhedrin contained all the groups opposed to Jesus.

Although, according to Mark, the Sanhedrin condemned Jesus to death, it is not certain that it had the right to order executions. The fact that Jesus was taken to Pilate before execution suggests that the Romans might not have allowed the Jews to impose the death penalty. (The Sanhedrin might, of course, have wanted to place the blame for Jesus' death on the Romans.) Also the method of execution laid down in the Law of Moses for blasphemy is death by stoning not crucifixion. The latter was a Roman punishment not a Jewish one.

The meeting of the Sanhedrin at the High Priest's house during the night was against its own rules. It should have met in the temple after daybreak.

The Sanhedrin came to an end with the destruction of the temple in AD 70.

e. References to Jesus' conflict with authority

2:1–3:6
3:22
7:1–13
8:11–13
10:2–12
11:15–19, 27–33
12:12, 13–17, 18–27, 38–40
14:1–2, 10–11, 43, 53–65
15:1–15, 31

Questions for chapter 7

1. 2:1–12
   (a) Describe how the paralysed man was brought to Jesus.
   (b) What did Jesus first say to him?
   (c) Why did the lawyers object to this?
   (d) What did Jesus say next and what happened?

2. 2:15–26
   Give three examples of the objections the Pharisees raised against Jesus and the disciples.

3. 3:1–6
   (a) Why did the Pharisees think it wrong of Jesus to heal the man with the withered arm?
   (b) What did Jesus ask them and what did they do after he had healed the man?

4. 12:18–27
   (a) What question did the Sadducees ask Jesus?
   (b) What reply did Jesus give?
   (c) How did the Sadducees' question reflect their beliefs?

5. Trace the course of the opposition to Jesus in *either* (a) the early chapters of Mark's gospel; *or* (b) after Jesus' arrival in Jerusalem.

6. How did the early church account for the persecution it suffered?

8. Jesus' purpose according to Mark

a. A new idea of Messiahship

(i) Preaching and healing: prophecy fulfilled

Jesus spent his life demonstrating what it meant to be the Messiah. He had a new idea of Messiahship and he made himself a living example of this idea.

The traditional belief was that the Messiah would bring about the rule of God by force. There was to be a kingdom ruled by God and only the Jews and those Gentiles willing to accept conversion were to be admitted to it.

Where this kingdom was to be established was not clear. Some thought of an earthly state with Jerusalem at its centre, while others thought it would come into being in the future when the deserving dead would be resurrected and rewarded. This was the background against which Jesus had to establish his idea.

In the early part of the gospel Mark shows Jesus healing and teaching. The two activities were closely connected. Both had to be 'understood'. His teaching could only be understood if 'you had ears to hear': that is, if you had faith. Those without faith would hear the words Jesus spoke but not understand their importance.

It was the same with the healings. Those without faith would see the healings but not understand that they were signs. They showed that God was fulfilling prophecy through Jesus. Mark believed that the prophet Isaiah was writing about the coming of the Messiah when he prophesied that the blind would see, the deaf hear, the lame walk, the dumb speak and the poor would have the gospel preached to them (Isa. 35:5–6; 61:1).

When Mark shows Jesus beginning his teaching by saying, 'the kingdom of God is upon you' (1:15), Mark is emphasising that the kingdom is present wherever Jesus is. Where the Messiah is, there is the kingdom of God. The blind, deaf, lame and dumb are healed and the good news is preached.

Jesus shows what things will be like when the rule of God is established. This is what Mark's church was waiting and working for – the establishment of God's kingdom throughout the world.

The meaning of the preaching and healing is understood by Peter. When Jesus asks, 'Who do you say I am?' Peter replies, 'You are the Messiah' (8:27–33). This is the climax of the first half of Mark's gospel. The faith of the disciples and the church is confirmed. Jesus accepts the title but demands secrecy. (For the theme of secrecy in Mark's gospel see chapter 4 c.)

(ii) The new Messiah

Immediately after Peter has called Jesus Messiah, Mark places the first statement of what Jesus understands the title to mean. Instead of talking about rewards for the faithful and glory for the Messiah, Jesus begins to teach that 'the Son of Man (Messiah) had to undergo great sufferings' (8:31).

This was the new idea of Messiahship Jesus had come to teach. He is to be a Messiah who suffers, serves and rises from the dead. These three themes recur time and time again when Jesus speaks of his mission and what it means to follow him.

All this is too new for Peter to accept it. He protests, and is told that he thinks like men, not as God thinks (8:32–33). He must learn that there is to be no glory in this world for the disciples of the Messiah. The old dreams of a supreme conqueror must be forgotten, and instead of a sword his followers must take up a cross (8:34–38).

This prophecy of suffering, and the transfiguration which follows, mark a turning point in the gospel. From now on Jesus is shown teaching about the sort of Messiah he is and what it means to be his disciple.

Mark illustrates the three themes of serving, suffering and resurrection which make up this new idea of Messiahship by describing incidents in which Jesus instructs his disciples.

1. Serving. The disciples find it hard to shake off their old ideas. Twice Mark shows them worrying about who is

the greatest. The first time the argument involves all the disciples, the second James and John ask Jesus for positions of honour in his kingdom (9:33–35; 10:35–45). In each case Jesus replies by teaching about serving others. Greatness is not found in ruling, but in being a willing servant to all. The disciples are still thinking like men, while Jesus is holding before them the idea of a Messiah who serves.

2. Suffering. When James and John ask for positions of honour Jesus responds by promising them suffering like that which he must face. 'The cup that I drink you shall drink' (10:39). The promise means that those who faithfully follow Jesus and live in obedience to God's will are sure to suffer in this evil world. In the end, though, the reward of the kingdom of God will be theirs.

Mark combines these two themes when he shows Jesus explaining that he is 'to give up his life as a ransom for many' (10:45). Jesus' service to his followers extends even as far as death, so that they can be saved.

3. Resurrection. Each time that Jesus says that the Son of Man must suffer and die he goes on to talk about being raised from the dead. (See 8:31; 9:31; 10:33–34.) The disciples do not understand what he means; the conquest of death is beyond their imagining. But, if Jesus is to fulfil God's plan and defeat evil in his new way, he must show that he has faith that he will bring about the kingdom of God by serving, suffering, dying and rising again.

At the Last Supper, Jesus uses the bread and wine as symbols for what is to happen to him and to his disciples who become one with him by sharing in the meal. Then the prophecies are fulfilled. Jesus is arrested, suffers, dies and rises again. Since death does not have the power to hold him, his new idea of Messiahship triumphs. The suffering servant has shown a new way to defeat evil and save mankind.

Jesus' idea of what it meant to be the Messiah led to a new understanding of how one could enter the kingdom of God. No longer was it reserved for Jews alone. Anyone who was willing to follow Jesus could enter.

b. The Transfiguration 9:2–8

The transfiguration is probably the strangest incident in the gospel. Not by accident, Mark places it at the centre of his account of the good news. It comes immediately after two important events – Peter's confession that Jesus is the Messiah, and Jesus' explanation of his new idea of Messiahship.

It is impossible now to recover the details of the experience Peter, James and John underwent. What we can do is to try to understand what this event meant to Mark. If we examine each part of his description we can begin to see how many ideas he compressed into a few lines.

To be transfigured means to be transformed or changed in appearance. The change affected Jesus' clothes as well as his face. They became a dazzling white 'no bleacher on earth could equal'.

It was a popular belief of that time that those chosen to live in the kingdom of God would be given new bodies and radiant garments. If the whiteness was not of this world, then Mark's readers would understand it was the radiance of God's kingdom. What the disciples were seeing was a vision of Jesus as he would be at his Second Coming, when he returned in glory to rule the kingdom of God.

Next Elijah and Moses appear. It was believed in Jesus' time that famous figures from the Old Testament would reappear when the present world drew to a close. The disciples discuss this with Jesus immediately after the transfiguration (9:9–13).

Elijah was expected to prepare the way for the Messiah and Mark opens his gospel by presenting John the Baptist as the Elijah who had been prophesied. At the transfiguration, Elijah is accompanied by Moses, another figure expected to herald the end. The appearance of these two indicated to Mark's readers that the present age was coming to its end, and that Jesus was the one chosen by God to bring in the new age.

The three disciples are scared by the vision and Peter asks, 'Shall we make three shelters?' He asks this, Mark says, because they were so terrified they did not know what to say.

Peter's question, however, is not just terrified nonsense. It seems to arise out of a belief that at the end of time God

74

would live among his chosen people again, as he had during their wanderings in the wilderness. The rough shelters they had used then were a symbol of this hope. So Peter seems to be asking, 'Is this the end of time and is God to live among us once more?'

Then a cloud appears, casts its shadow over them and a voice comes from it. The scene is similar to the occasions when God spoke to Moses (e.g. Exod. 24:16–18). The mountain, the cloud and the voice all indicate that the circumstances are those in which God chooses to reveal his will to men.

The voice says, 'This is my Son, my Beloved; listen to him.' It echoes the voice at Jesus' baptism, this time adding 'listen to him'. What had Jesus said? Immediately before this Mark has placed Jesus' first statement of what it meant to be the Messiah – suffering, death, resurrection. The voice from the cloud confirms that Jesus is expressing God's will: the Messiah is to be one who suffers and serves.

When the cloud vanishes the three disciples are left with Jesus alone. The way Mark has written this adds another meaning to the instruction 'listen to him'. Elijah and Moses represent the prophets and the Law of the Old Testament. These were the channels through which God had previously revealed his will to his chosen people. Now they vanish and only Jesus is left. Listen to him. He is to be the one in future to reveal God's will.

Mark's account of the vision ends with Jesus surrounded by the nucleus of his church, Peter, James and John.

The transfiguration has shown three things – Jesus in glory; Jesus heralded by Elijah and Moses; and authority transferred from the Law and the prophets to Jesus and his church. That was its importance for Mark and why he made it the central point of his gospel.

c. Mark's use of titles

Son of Man

The title 'Son of Man' is the most popular messianic title in Mark's gospel and the one Jesus uses of himself. For Mark, and so far as we can tell for Jesus himself, the title referred to one who acted with God's authority.

The words 'son of man' were, to start with, a Hebrew expression which meant 'man'. If you are a son of man then quite simply you are a man. This was how the phrase was used in the psalms.

It gathered new meaning when it was used in Daniel. This book was probably written during the second century BC, a period of persecution for the Jews, and was designed to encourage them to remain faithful to their religion.

In chapter 7 Daniel tells of a vision he experienced. In it he saw four terrible beasts, an old man, and one like a son of man. The interpretation of the vision explains that the beasts were the kingdoms which oppressed God's people, the old man (the Ancient in Years) was God, and the son of man was one who represented the saints of the Most High (God). The vision foretold that the saints of the Most High would suffer for a time under the rule of the kingdoms, then judgment would be given by God in favour of those who had remained faithful in spite of persecution, and 'kingly power, sovereignty, and greatness of all the kingdoms under heaven' would be given to them (Dan. 7:27).

The son of man was a representative of the faithful people of God. When Mark shows Jesus using this title he does so in the way it was used in Daniel. The son of man is to be a faithful servant of God, and to win his 'kingly power' not by force of arms but by suffering because of his obedience to God's will.

When Jesus talks about himself, he uses this title not Messiah, and when Peter first calls him Messiah Jesus immediately speaks of the Son of Man to emphasise the suffering and to remove any idea that he may be a conquering king.

Mark believed that by taking this title, Jesus was saying that those who followed him, and suffered yet remained faithful, would be like the saints of the Most High in Daniel. When judgment was given they would share in the kingly power which was to be given to the Son of Man.

The title combined four main ideas – that of a man who acted with God's authority; of people perfectly faithful to God; of one who suffers as a result of such faithfulness; and of a future when the faithful would be rewarded. Mark may have had all of these ideas in mind as he wrote.

76

References to the title Son of Man, 2:10, 28; 8:31; 9:9, 31; 10:33; 13:26; 14:21, 41.

Son of God

Mark opens his gospel by saying, 'Here begins the gospel of Jesus Christ the Son of God.' At the crucifixion a Roman soldier says, 'Truly this man was a son of God.' Since Mark uses this title to open his account of Jesus' ministry and to comment on his death, he clearly thought it important.

In Hebrew to call someone a son of something meant that he had that characteristic (e.g. James and John are called Sons of Thunder). The title shows that Jesus had the characteristics of God, he was like God. Jesus does not refer to himself by this title, it is a comment on him by his followers and by the demons who recognise his true nature.

In Matthew's gospel one of the Beatitudes runs, 'How blest are the peacemakers; God shall call them his sons' (Matt. 5:9). It appears that anyone who followed Jesus' teaching would be behaving as God wished and so be a son of God.

In Matthew and Luke the title is also taken to mean son in the human sense. The conception of Jesus by Mary is described in such a way as to suggest that he was son of God through the action of the Holy Spirit in place of a human father. This was a Gentile rather than a Jewish understanding of the title son of God.

Mark's use of the title is closer to the Jewish. His introduction seems to mean that he is going to tell the good news of Jesus Christ who behaved on earth entirely in obedience to God's will. This obedience is recognised by the soldier's words at the crucifixion. The implication is that anyone who did the same would also deserve the title because he would be displaying god-like qualities.

References to the title Son of God, 1:1, 11; 3:11; 5:7; 9:7; 13:32; 14:61; 15:39.

Son of David

'Son of David' is a title for the Messiah. It meant that the Messiah would be a king like David – who was regarded by the Jews as an ideal ruler – and that the Messiah would be from among David's descendants. Both Matthew and Luke trace Jesus' descent from David.

Mark does not do this, but makes use of the title in a different way. Bartimaeus, a blind beggar, shouts out the title publicly, but Jesus does not tell him to be silent as he has others who recognised his true identity. Mark places this incident at the point in the gospel where Jesus turns towards Jerusalem (10:46). By accepting the title Jesus seems to be saying that the time for secrecy is past. He is going openly to meet his enemies.

The other place in Mark where the title appears is when Jesus is teaching in the temple (12:35–37). He points out that in Psalm 110 David, who was believed to have written it, calls the Messiah 'Lord' which he would not do if the Messiah was one of his descendants and so his junior. The meaning of this strange discussion seems to be that the Messiah is no ordinary king but greater than any in the past.

References to the title Son of David, 10:47; 12:35, 37.

Messiah or Christ

Both these words mean 'the anointed one'. 'Messiah' is Hebrew and 'Christ' is Greek. The reason Jesus has titles in both languages is that his first followers were Jews, but the international language of the first century was Greek and it was in that language that the New Testament was written.

In the Old Testament anointing meant having oil poured over your head (e.g. 1 Sam. 10:1). It was equivalent to being crowned and showed that the person had been adopted by God as his son, and chosen to be king of God's people. The king had the duty of representing the people before God and of conveying God's will to the people. There was, among the Hebrews, less distinction between the duties of priest and king than there is today.

It was believed by the Jews of Jesus' day that God would send his Messiah to free them from oppression and set up a government which would rule in accordance with God's laws. Many thought this would be accomplished by force, and in Mark the title seems to be connected with the idea of a conquering king. When Peter calls Jesus 'Messiah', Jesus immediately starts to use the title 'Son of Man' which does not have military overtones.

Jesus only claims the title publicly when on trial before the High Priest. Until then he has kept his identity a secret. (See chapter 4 c. for a suggestion as to why it is revealed at this point.)

References to the title Messiah or Christ, 8:29; 9:41; 14:61.

Questions for chapter 8

1. 8:27–9:1
   (a) Describe the conversation which took place on the road to Caesarea Philippi.
   (b) Why did Jesus call Peter 'Satan'?
   (c) What did Jesus teach about following him?

2. 10:35–45
   (a) What favour did James and John ask for?
   (b) What did Jesus reply?
   (c) How did the other disciples react and what did Jesus teach them?

3. 9:2–8
   (a) Describe the transfiguration.
   (b) What was its importance for Mark and his church?

4. Why does Jesus use the title 'Son of Man' to describe himself rather than 'Messiah'?

5. How do the disciples react to Jesus' prophecies concerning the death and resurrection of the Son of Man?

6. What is new about Jesus' idea of Messiahship? Give two or three examples from Mark's gospel to illustrate your answer.

9.   The miracles of Jesus

a. What is a miracle?

No doubt you would think it strange if someone asked when you last saw or experienced a miracle. After all, we live in a world where we do not expect miracles to happen as part of the daily routine. Yet the idea is not strange to us. We all have a good idea of what a miracle is.

There are people today who claim to have had direct experience of miracles. The Bible contains many miracle stories, though miracles are by no means confined to the Bible. They are common in other religions and cultures as well. In fact it would not be an exaggeration to say that the idea of miracles is as old as man himself.

The common view of miracle is that it is something which goes against the laws of nature. Our world is largely explained in scientific terms. We expect things to happen according to certain 'rules' and for certain reasons. Miracles appear to contradict reason and therefore most of us are reluctant to accept them. We would at least first try to find reasons to explain whatever it is that was claimed to be a miracle. Even if we could not work out a reason, the most sceptical of us would still reject the miracle on the grounds that there must be a scientific answer but we have not thought of it!

b. Did Jesus perform miracles?

This chapter is about the miracles which Mark claims Jesus performed. In the twentieth century, the miracles are perhaps the most difficult part of Jesus' life and work to understand. Many people find they can accept Jesus' message but not his miracles. They might justifiably ask, 'How can people with the ability to reason and with the benefit of scientific knowledge, accept what Mark tells us about a man who cures the sick, stills a storm and walks on water?' We can perhaps sympathise with this point of view. But, in fairness to Mark, we ought to ask a number of other questions. For example, did the people who lived in the first century AD believe in miracles? Did they know about our 'laws of nature'? Was Jesus the only person in the ancient world who performed miracles? What is Mark trying to tell us when he casts Jesus in the role of miracle-worker?

This chapter does not set out to try to prove beyond doubt that the miracles of Jesus really happened. Nor does it attempt to disprove them. Both would be impossible tasks. It does set out to examine the answers to some of the questions we have just raised, and to try to uncover something of Mark's purpose in writing.

c. Miracles and magic in the first century AD

(i) A world filled with spirits

If we are to understand anything at all about the miracles of which Mark speaks, we must look at them against the background of the first century AD. Something has already been said about the beliefs of the time (chapter 4) but it will be as well to remind ourselves once again.

Many people then believed that the world was subject to the actions of spirits which might work for man or against him. These spirits were thought to live in the air. The evil ones haunted lonely places such as ruins and tombs. Man was thought to be under constant threat from them because they frequently attacked people and entered their bodies. Any event which could not be readily explained was attributed to the activities of the spirit world.

It is very easy for us to mock this idea because we have been conditioned to a scientific outlook. However, had we lived in the first century AD, we can be sure that we too would have believed in spirits!

(ii) Spirits and illness

When people were ill or suffering in some way the usual explanation was that it was the work of an evil spirit or demon. The patient was thought to be possessed by the demon. Medicine, as we know it, did not exist. People with the power to heal used a strange blend of medicine and magic in their methods. The object was to drive out the evil spirit which was causing the affliction, and so restore the patient to good health.

Demons were thought to be extremely hostile and so the job of the exorcist (that is, the person who drives out the evil spirit) was a dangerous one. He had to use force on occasions and, if he was to be completely successful, he needed also to know the name of the demon or the type he was dealing with so that he could assert his superiority and authority over it.

In addition to causing physical and mental harm, demons also caused people to behave badly and do evil things. They would seek especially to turn people away from God.

Those skilled in the art of healing would use a variety of methods in their cures including magical words and phrases as well as actions and the application of potions.

Superstition, fear and dread of the unknown were commonplace in the world of the first century AD. Magicians and wonder-workers were held in high esteem because it was they who could help when the demon struck. Just as we go to the doctor when we are ill so the people of the first century would seek out a magician to obtain a cure.

d. Mark and miracles

When we come to look more closely at the miracles in Mark's gospel, we will see that this is the background against which he writes. This is not to say that he presents Jesus as some sort of magician, he does not. But there are traces of magic in Mark and we will be able to uncover these in due course. (See detailed notes in chapter 10.)

It may be that the methods Jesus had used in his cures were largely forgotten. Mark, writing for people who were living in a different culture and in a different generation from that of Jesus, may have decided to clothe the miracles with detail that would be readily appreciated and understood by his readers. Remember, Mark wrote his gospel for the persecuted Christians of Rome and he adapted the message to suit the needs and interests of those people. They felt themselves under the threat not only of the pagan empire but of the demons who lurked in the air waiting to attack and enter the body. In Jesus they had a divine wonder-worker who could save them from the evil which they might encounter at any time.

The miraculous was so much a part of Mark's world that he would not have been faced with the same problems of belief that we experience today. He would not have dreamt of asking such a question as, 'Did Jesus really perform miracles?' If Jesus was God's Son then of course he must have done.

e. Symbolism in the miracles

In chapter 5 we saw how Mark uses symbols to make clear his meaning about baptism. The miracles, which incidentally occupy almost one third of Mark's gospel, are also full of symbolism. Again we will need to use detective-style methods to uncover Mark's full meaning, and we must not necessarily accept what he says at face value.

As we read Mark's gospel we must keep constantly in mind his belief about the death and resurrection of Jesus. For Mark, the resurrection was *the greatest miracle* the world had ever known. Jesus' death had appeared to be a triumph for evil but, in raising Jesus from the dead, God had won his final victory. The resurrection of Jesus was what inspired Mark to write. All that he says is written in the light of this event and is totally influenced by it. The miracles of which he speaks are but reflections of *the great miracle*. Some of them, not surprisingly, suggest the raising from the dead. For example, the Gerasene demoniac (who lived among the dead), Jairus' daughter (Jesus was told that he was too late, the girl was already dead), and the epileptic boy (he lay on the ground as if he were dead).

You will see many more examples of Mark's use of symbols when you study the individual miracle stories and read the detailed comments in chapter 10.

f. Jesus and the fight against evil

Immediately after his baptism, Jesus was said to have been driven by the Spirit (that is, God's Holy Spirit) into the wilderness to be tempted by Satan (Satan was the prince of demons and represented all that was evil). For Mark, that was the beginning of a long struggle between Satan and

Jesus. But it was only the beginning because, throughout the gospel, Jesus meets up with the forces of evil (represented by the demons). He defeats them time and again and so proves victorious over them. But the struggle ends only when Jesus conquers death at the resurrection.

Mark wanted to ensure that his readers fully understood the significance of Jesus' miracles. They represented the triumph of good over evil. Each cure performed by Jesus was another nail in Satan's coffin. Yet, not everyone understood what Jesus was doing. Even his family and friends were sometimes blind to the truth. At 3:19b–27, Mark tells how Jesus' friends mistakenly supposed that he himself was possessed by demons (to be beside oneself or to be out of one's mind was to be under the power of demons). The lawyers or scribes suggested that Jesus was in league with Satan (Beelzebub is another name for Satan) and that he was using demonic power to perform miracles.

Jesus replied to his critics in two short parables. He pointed out that if his power was from Satan then it would mean that Satan's kingdom was in a state of civil war, because Jesus' aim was to cure people while Satan's aim was to make them ill or mad. (A kingdom fighting itself will collapse.)

The second parable emphasises that Jesus and Satan are on opposite sides. It says that you cannot rob a strong man unless you have first overpowered him and tied him up. Here the strong man represents Satan and Jesus is the robber. In curing people Jesus is robbing Satan of his power. To be able to do that he must first have overpowered and bound Satan. Clearly, then, Jesus is the stronger of the two. The only power stronger than Satan's comes from God.

Mark follows these two parables by giving a stern warning (vv. 28–30) to all who would doubt Jesus' real identity and purpose. It is unforgivable to accuse Jesus of being in league with Satan. The power Jesus displays is none other than the power of God's Holy Spirit. Whoever speaks against such a power will not be forgiven.

g. Mark's theme of secrecy and revelation

As this theme has already received detailed comment earlier (chapter 4) we will do no more here than remind ourselves of it. It is a theme which crops up with amazing regularity in the miracles as elsewhere in the gospel, and it is important to remember Mark's possible motives in using it.

So that you have a clear understanding of what these motives were, it would be a good idea, before looking in detail at the miracle stories, to re-read the section on page 30 entitled 'Jesus the unrecognised Messiah'.

Questions for chapter 9

1. What beliefs did people of the first century AD hold about the cause of illness?

2. What is exorcism?

3. How did the exorcist go about his work?

4. What would Mark have considered to be the greatest miracle?

5. Jesus was accused by the lawyers of being in league with Satan. How does Mark explain that this is *not* true?

10. The miracles as told by Mark

a. Types of miracle in Mark

We turn now to examine the text of the individual miracle
stories in Mark's gospel. These will be looked at in three
separate categories – the exorcisms; the healing miracles;
the nature miracles. We must, however, be on our guard
because in viewing the miracles out of the context of the
gospel as a whole we are in danger of losing the aim and
intention of the writer. It is not by accident that the miracle
stories are placed where they are in Mark's gospel and
frequently they serve more than one purpose. For example,
the story of the healing of the man with the withered arm
(at 3:1–6) is important in the context of Jesus' conflict with
the Pharisees (as you will have seen in chapter 7) and it also
illustrates the teaching of Jesus concerning attitudes towards
the Sabbath. In fact it would seem that these aspects are
more important to Mark than the healing itself.

In dividing the miracles into three separate groups we
also need to take care. Mark would not have recognised the
distinctions we make. For example, it is dangerous to make
too clear a distinction between the exorcisms and healings
which Jesus performed. In those days illness of any shape
or form was thought to be either the result of demon possession or as punishment for sin. In either case the suffering
was the direct result of something evil.

Some notes will be given on each miracle to aid study.

b. The exorcisms

The following passages should be studied in conjunction
with this section,

(i) The man with the unclean spirit 1:21–28
(ii) The Gerasene demoniac 5:1–20
(iii) The daughter of the Syrophoenician woman 7:24–30
(iv) The epileptic boy 9:14–29

(i) The man with the unclean spirit 1:21–28

1. The evil spirit in the man instantly recognises Jesus and calls him by name, 'the Holy One of God'. Mark is making the point that Jesus operates in a spiritual as well as a human dimension. Whereas the people were astonished and amazed at Jesus, the spirit world immediately recognised him as the Messiah. This is an example of the theme of secrecy and revelation which Mark uses in his gospel.

2. To gain complete mastery over your opponent in exorcism, it was thought to be necessary to know his name – hence the evil spirit uses both Jesus' earthly title, 'Jesus of Nazareth', and a title for the Messiah, 'Holy One of God', but to no effect. This emphasises that the power of God is stronger than the power of Satan.

3. The aspect of horror and violence which accompanied exorcism is made clear in verse 26.

(ii) The Gerasene demoniac 5:1–20

1. The description of the man and his condition is worthy of attention. He lives among the dead, is unbelievably strong (no human power can hold him) and completely insane (the name Legion suggests that he was a very severe case indeed, possessed by many demons).

2. The evil spirits again instantly recognise Jesus and refer to him as 'Son of the Most High God'. Jesus too asks the man's name presumably to gain power over the demons.

3. Apart from the horrific description of the possessed man, this story is best remembered because of the loss of pigs. We miss the point completely, however, if we start to ask such questions as, 'Why did Jesus allow animals to suffer in this way?' The point of this part of the story is to prove that the demons really had left the man and so confirm the miracle. It was also a commonly held belief that exorcised demons would take revenge, and this loss of pigs (demons were believed to live in animals as well as humans) illustrates well their spiteful and destructive nature. They were certainly a force to be reckoned with. No doubt the early hearers of this story would have been led to ask, 'Who is this who has so much of God's power at his disposal?' And

that is the question Mark answers time and again in his gospel.

4. The theme of secrecy and revelation appears again in this story. Jesus' true identity is apparent to the demons yet remains a secret from the people who, at verse 17, beg Jesus to leave their neighbourhood. They have completely failed to recognise who Jesus really is. However, the order of Jesus to the cured man is unusual in that Jesus tells him to spread the news of his cure. Elsewhere in Mark, Jesus tries to persuade people to keep their cure a secret. The probable reason is that here Jesus is on Gentile ground not Jewish ('the country of the Gerasenes', where the people kept pigs, a thing Jews were forbidden to do) and Mark's rule about secrecy seems not to apply.

5. Mark probably intended his readers to interpret this story as a raising from the dead. He emphasises that Legion's home is a graveyard – the place of dead men. After the cure, however, the change is remarkable. The man is seated and clothed and wants to be with Jesus, and at verse 20 is found proclaiming the good news. From being under the total influence of Satan he is now actively engaged in the fight against him. He has, in other words, overcome death.

6. We have already noted that this incident is placed in Gentile territory. Mark perhaps wishes to emphasise that Jesus' ministry was not just for the Jews alone but for non-Jews also – an important point if you are writing for Gentile Christians.

(iii) The daughter of the Syrophoenician woman 7:24–30

1. In this miracle story emphasis is placed on the dialogue between Jesus and the woman rather than on the cure itself. Jesus does not come into direct conflict with the troublesome demon and apparently rids the girl of it from a distance.

2. The incident took place outside Jewish territory, but Mark makes the point that even so Jesus' presence could not be kept a secret.

3. The dialogue between Jesus and the woman is puzzling. She was a non-Jew and Jesus' reply makes it clear

that his work was strictly for the Jews – 'the children' equals Jews, 'the dogs' equals non-Jews. The woman's answer, which suggested that the food for both came from the same source, got her what she wanted, namely the casting out of the demon.

4. We might ask, 'Why does Mark present Jesus as so reluctant to help someone who was not a Jew?' 'Why was he so insulting?' To call someone a dog is very insulting (indeed, the supreme insult in the east), even if the Greek word does suggest a household pet rather than a scavenger. We can only speculate, but it could be Mark's way of emphasising that Jesus was the Messiah foretold in the Old Testament, and thus, a very Jewish character indeed. As such his sole concern would have been for the Jews and their well-being. Also the needs of the early church may have helped shape the story. For some time the early Christians believed that the gospel should be preached first to Jews then to Gentiles. This story might have been used to show that Jesus himself approved this pattern. Of course, it could also have been used to favour the mission to the Gentiles, in that Jesus did cure the girl after the mother had pointed out that non-Jews could also benefit from Jewish good fortune.

(iv) The epileptic boy 9:14–29

1. This story is as much about faith (or the lack of it) as Jesus' ability to exorcise a demon. When told that his disciples are unable to drive out the evil spirit, Jesus speaks against the whole generation for its lack of faith. His words are characteristic of the laments of the Old Testament prophets. Even after Jesus' words the father suggests that the demon may be too powerful for Jesus by saying, 'if it is at all possible . . . help us' (v.22). Jesus repeats his words, 'If it is possible!' and then says that all things are possible to those who have faith. The words of the father are some of the best known in the New Testament, 'I have faith; help me where faith falls short' (v. 24), and no doubt gave comfort to the members of Mark's community who felt that their faith in God was sometimes inadequate. The story shows that if you have faith, however weak, even the most hopeless of situations can be resolved.

2. The condition of the boy is described in vivid detail – see verses 18, 20, 22 and 26. So serious is this case of possession that Jesus' disciples are unable to drive out the demon. Only Jesus is able to do this.

3. The demon reacts violently to Jesus' presence, presumably indicating that it knows who Jesus really is. As a result of the exorcism the boy is left for dead. Jesus immediately takes him by the hand and raises him up. This is undoubtedly a symbol of Jesus' own death and resurrection, especially as the incident is placed between the first and second predictions which Jesus makes about his future sufferings and death (see 8:31 and 9:31).

4. Mark adds a postscript to this story which aims to emphasise the need for prayer if exorcisms are to be performed successfully. As this does not appear to have been an original part of the story, we might assume that Mark is writing of the experiences of the early church.

5. Finally, it is important to note that this miracle occurs immediately after the transfiguration (see chapter 8 for explanation of this) in which Jesus' mission and purpose is confirmed. This story provides an acted out example of what the function of the Messiah is, namely to restore the faithful to life.

Questions on the exorcisms

1. 1:21–28
    (a) What did the unclean spirit say to Jesus?
    (b) How did the people react to the healing?
    (c) Why did the demon recognise Jesus but the people did not?

2. 5:1–20
    (a) Where did this incident take place?
    (b) Describe Legion and his condition.
    (c) What happened when the evil spirits left the man?
    (d) Describe Legion *after* the exorcism.
    (e) Why, do you suppose, did the people want Jesus to leave their country?

3. 7:24–30
    (a) What nationality was the woman?
    (b) What reply did Jesus give to the woman's request?
    (c) What did the woman mean when she said, ' . . . even
        the dogs under the table eat the children's scraps'?
    (d) Why, do you suppose, did Mark make Jesus appear
        reluctant to heal the girl?

4. 9:14–29
    (a) Describe the condition of the boy.
    (b) What reply did the father give when Jesus said,
        'Everything is possible to one who has faith'?
    (c) What did people think had happened to the boy
        immediately after the exorcism?
    (d) Why were the disciples unable to perform the
        exorcism?
    (e) Mark undoubtedly saw this as a death/resurrection
        story. Why did he place it at this point in his gospel?

c. The healings

The following passages should be studied in conjunction
with this section.

(i) Simon's mother-in-law   1:29–31
(ii) The healing of the leper   1:40–45
(iii) The healing of the paralytic   2:1–12
(iv) The man with the withered arm   3:1–6
(v) Jairus' daughter   5:21–24, 35–43
(vi) The woman with the haemorrhage   5:24–34
(vii) The deaf stammerer   7:31–37
(viii) The blind man of Bethsaida   8:22–26
(ix) Blind Bartimaeus   10:46–52
(x) Mass healings and exorcisms   1:32–34; 3:10–12;
    6:53–56

(i) Simon's mother-in-law 1:29–31

1. Mark gives only the bare bones of this miracle. Apparently no word is spoken by Jesus; he takes her by the hand
and lifts her up.

2. The completeness of the cure and its miraculous speed is suggested by the words, ' . . . and she waited upon them' (v. 31).

(ii) The healing of the leper 1:40–45

1. Sufferers of the terrible disease of leprosy were certain of two things – that they would die a slow and disfiguring death, and that they would experience permanent separation from their families and from society once the priest had pronounced them unclean.

2. To touch the man as Jesus did would have been unthinkable because leprosy is a contagious disease. Mark, however, stresses that Jesus is prepared to help the outcast from Jewish society.

3. Mark uses his favourite secrecy/revelation theme. Jesus tells the man not to tell anyone about his cure, but the message cannot be contained as verse 45 shows.

4. Jesus also instructs the man to obey the Law by reporting to a priest to be pronounced clean and to make sacrifice (as specified in Leviticus 14).

(iii) The healing of the paralytic 2:1–12

1. Mark uses this incident to show how Jesus came into conflict with the Jewish authorities almost from the start of his ministry. (See chapter 7.)

2. The real point of the story is to do with Jesus' authority to forgive sins. The early Christians believed that Jesus was Messiah and as such had the power of God at his disposal. They believed that sin could be forgiven by and through Jesus. To the Jews who did not accept the Messiahship of Jesus, the claim to be able to forgive sins was simply blasphemous (that is, it was speaking against God). They believed that God alone could forgive sin.

3. If sin caused illness then to forgive sin or to pronounce a cure amounted to the same thing. There is the suggestion in the story that it is easier to say that the man's sins are forgiven than it is actually to get him to walk, therefore if the latter is achieved then the former should also be believed.

4. There is no suggestion of secrecy in this story. Quite the opposite in fact, as Jesus declares himself to be Son of Man – a title which here stands for Messiah. (See chapter 8.)

5. Jesus is again shown to be capable of operating in a different dimension. The lawyers do not actually voice their objections yet Jesus is able to know what they are thinking.

6. The faith of the man and his friends is recognised by Jesus and the completeness of the cure is stressed (he takes up his bed and walks to the amazement of all).

(iv) The man with the withered arm 3:1–6

1. The conflict between Jesus and the Jewish authorities on the use of the Sabbath is the main issue of this incident (see chapter 7 for further comment and especially for reference to verse 6); the miracle itself plays a subsidiary role.

2. The Jewish Law would allow help to be given on the Sabbath only if life was in danger. In this case it was apparently not a matter of life or death.

3. The point Jesus makes is that it is more important to do good when the opportunity arises than blindly to obey a law.

(v) Jairus' daughter 5:21–24, 35–43

1. This miracle story shows that Jesus' power extends even to raising people from the dead. Though Jesus says the girl is only sleeping, it is clear that Mark intended the incident as a raising from the dead. Christians often referred to the dead as sleeping because of their belief that the dead would be awakened at the resurrection.

2. Usually the Jewish religious leaders are in opposition to Jesus, but here Jairus comes to Jesus and begs for his help. The girl is at the point of death and only someone with supernatural powers can save her.

3. Faith is an important element of the story. Jairus shows faith in coming to Jesus in the first place and when the news comes that his daughter is already dead Jesus urges Jairus to continue to believe. The messengers do not possess this faith; they suggest that Jesus should not be troubled further.

The professional mourners who are at the house do not have faith; they laugh at Jesus.

4. Mark, writing in Greek, quotes the actual Aramaic words which Jesus speaks, '*Talitha cum*'. These words were perhaps preserved by the early church because they were thought to have special power. Wonder-workers of Mark's day often used foreign phrases as part of their magic.

5. We are made aware that the cure is complete. The girl gets up, walks about and is in need of food.

6. The command to secrecy is again given, though in this instance it would seem rather pointless as the news could hardly be contained.

(vi) The woman with the haemorrhage 5:24–34

1. It was a common belief in the ancient world that anything associated with a healer had power in itself. The woman (who had apparently spent a fortune on medical advice to no effect) believed that Jesus had such great power that simply to touch his clothes would cure her. What she believed actually happened.

2. Somehow Jesus knew that power had gone from him, though his disciples did not understand what he meant. Eventually Jesus made personal contact with the woman. The miracle is confirmed because of the woman's faith.

(vii) The deaf stammerer 7:31–37

1. The methods which Mark says Jesus used to perform this cure are similar to those used by other Jewish and Greek healers of the time and suggest an element of magic. In particular the touching of the man's ears and tongue, the use of saliva which was thought to have healing powers, the look towards heaven and the sigh, and the use of the Aramaic word *Ephphatha* are all associated with magical practices. (See note 4 on the healing of Jairus' daughter for comment on the use of Aramaic.)

2. Mark makes a clever reference to the Old Testament to show that Jesus is the Messiah long awaited by the Jews. He uses a single Greek word which is translated in our Bibles as 'had an impediment in his speech'. The only place

in the Old Testament where this same word occurs is at Isaiah 35:6. Here there is a description of what will happen when the Messiah comes. It says that the blind will see, the deaf will hear and the dumb shall sing for joy (Isa. 35:5–6). We shall see that the two remaining miracles of healing in Mark deal with the blind seeing; this one deals with the curing of the deaf and dumb.

3. Mark continues with the theme of keeping Jesus' true identity a secret. Jesus takes the man aside privately (v.33) and tells witnesses to the cure not to tell anyone (v.36). All this is to no avail as the rest of verse 36 makes clear.

(viii) The blind man of Bethsaida 8:22–26

1. This incident is very similar in many ways to the healing of the deaf stammerer, especially in the methods used by Jesus (see comments 1 and 2 on that miracle).

2. The cure seems to have taken place in two stages which suggests that Jesus was not completely successful at the first attempt. Perhaps for that reason both Matthew and Luke leave this incident out of their gospels. However, Mark has probably arranged the story this way for a special reason. When you studied the chapter on the disciples you saw that Mark presents them as slow to understand the real truth about Jesus. They do not see clearly who he is, just as the man in the story only has partial sight before the complete cure. The real truth about Jesus comes to the disciples in stages. Seen in this way the story has a symbolic dimension which may not be apparent at first glance.

3. Before the cure Jesus takes the man out of the village and afterwards tells him to return home without telling anyone about it. This follows Mark's pattern of secrecy.

(ix) Blind Bartimaeus 10:46–52

1. This is the last of Mark's healing miracles and the first in which Jesus is publicly recognised as Messiah without any effort being made to keep this a secret. Bartimaeus openly calls Jesus 'Son of David', which is a title for Messiah.

2. Much interest focuses on the blind man himself. He persists in his attempt to gain Jesus' attention despite being

discouraged by the crowd. Jesus tells him that it is his faith which has cured him.

3. Mark undoubtedly regarded Bartimaeus as a model disciple. Perhaps he was contrasting him with Jesus' disciples who had their sight but were unable to see clearly who Jesus really was. This man did not possess sight, yet could see quite clearly that Jesus was the Messiah. Mark also says that Bartimaeus' response to the cure was to *follow* Jesus.

(x) Mass healings and exorcisms

In addition to the individual stories of healing and exorcism, Mark also mentions in three places instances of mass healings (these can be found at 1:32–34; 3:10–12; 6:53–56). These have been written by Mark to summarise the overall reaction of the ordinary people to Jesus and to act as link passages. There is no doubt for Mark that Jesus was popular with the crowds. They recognised his power for what it was even if the authorities did not. Wherever he went they flocked to see him, and they brought to him their sick in vast numbers. Mark suggests that simply to touch Jesus' clothing was sufficient for the cure to be obtained instantly.

The first two of these summaries also emphasise the theme of secrecy. The demons continue to recognise Jesus, calling him by name. But the secret must be kept and so they are ordered to be silent.

Questions on the healings

1. 1:29–31
   (a) Who was with Jesus when he entered the house?
   (b) What action did Jesus take?
   (c) What tells us that the cure was effective?

2. 1:40–45
   (a) What did the leper ask Jesus?
   (b) After the cure, why did Jesus tell the man to see a priest?
   (c) Why was the leper also an outcast?

3. 2:1–12
   (a) What action did the man's friends take when they found they could not get near Jesus?

(b) What did Jesus say to the paralytic which offended the lawyers?

(c) What is blasphemy?

(d) Who does Jesus declare himself to be in this story?

(e) How did the crowd react to the healing?

4. 3:1–6

(a) What question did Jesus ask the Pharisees?

(b) Why was Jesus angry and sad at their attitude?

(c) In healing the man, what message was Jesus trying to get across?

5. 5:21–24, 35–43

(a) What did Jairus say when he came to Jesus?

(b) What message came from Jairus' house?

(c) How did Jesus react to the news that the girl was dead?

(d) What does *Talitha cum* mean?

(e) Give an example of faith and lack of faith shown in this story.

6. 5:24–34

(a) Why did the woman touch Jesus' clothes?

(b) What was the result of this action?

(c) What did the disciples think of Jesus' question, 'Who touched my clothes?'?

(d) What did Jesus say to the woman?

7. 7:31–37

(a) Describe the method of healing used by Jesus in this story.

(b) What comment was made concerning Jesus?

(c) How does Mark explain to his readers that Jesus is the Messiah prophesied in the Old Testament? (See note 2.)

8. 8:22–26

(a) What action did Jesus take when the blind man was brought to him?

(b) What was the reply when Jesus asked the man if he could see anything?

(c) Why might this story have special symbolic significance in the gospel?

9. 10:46–52

(a) What special title did Bartimaeus give Jesus?
(b) How did the crowd react to Bartimaeus' shouting?
(c) What question did Jesus ask Bartimaeus?
(d) What was Bartimaeus' reply?
(e) What do you think was Mark's opinion of Bartimaeus?

d. The nature miracles

The nature miracles are perhaps the hardest of all to understand. We might argue that Jesus was a man who had a very strong personality and was able to convince sick people that they were well. (After all, faith healers are not uncommon even today.) But who can believe that the weather will obey someone's command? Mark firmly believed that God was the creator and controller of nature. As such he could manipulate the elements as he wished. Mark also firmly believed that Jesus was God's representative on earth and as such had God's power at his disposal. This would include the power to control the weather.

Read the comments on each miracle carefully and note how each story can be interpreted symbolically and still make sense.

The following passages should be studied in conjunction with this section,

(i)   The stilling of the storm 4:35–41
(ii) The feeding of the five thousand 6:30–44
(iii) Jesus walks on the water 6:45–52
(iv) The feeding of the four thousand 8:1–10
(v)   The cursing of the fig tree 11:12–14, 20–25

(i) The stilling of the storm 4:35–41

1. To ask, 'Did it really happen?' is to ask the wrong question. This is a story which was undoubtedly popular teaching material in the early church. It is full of symbolism and many valuable lessons could be learnt from it. It has been so adapted that it is impossible to tell what really happened.

2. Some background information is necessary in order to interpret the symbolism.

(a) In the Old Testament the sea is often used to represent evil and chaos. The sea was terrifying to the Jews who were by and large landlubbers. It was thought to be inhabited by evil powers. The psalms suggested that God alone is able to control the raging sea (e.g. Psa. 107:28–29).

(b) At times of trouble when no help seemed forthcoming, the Jews often spoke of God as asleep. There are a number of references in the Old Testament where God is called upon to 'wake up!' (e.g. Psa. 44:23).

(c) The ability to sleep peacefully was a sign of complete and perfect trust in God (e.g. Psa. 4:8).

3. Against this background, the meaning of the story begins to unfold.

(a) Jesus is seen to have perfect trust in God – he sleeps during a violent storm.

(b) The disciples call on Jesus to 'wake up!'. They lack faith and this perfect trust which Jesus displays.

(c) The words of Jesus, 'Hush! Be still!', mean literally 'be muzzled'. Jesus uses the same word elsewhere to control a demon. Mark may be implying that the raging sea was the work of demons. Certainly he meant his readers to understand that Jesus was God's agent – only God could control the sea.

4. This incident may have had particular meaning for Mark and his community. Their church was being tossed on the waves of persecution and suffering. Sometimes they may have felt that Jesus did not care about them, just as did the disciples on the lake. But they knew that even if their faith was weak (again, like that of the disciples) Jesus would deal with the evil which faced them.

5. The real point of the story is contained in the question asked by the disciples, 'Who can this be? Even the wind and the sea obey him.' This was the question Mark wanted his readers to face. There could be only one answer for Mark – this is the Son of God.

(ii) The feeding of the five thousand 6:30–44

1. This story would have been full of meaning for the early Christians because it calls to mind the Last Supper

and the Eucharist. The actions of Jesus in blessing and breaking the bread are the same as those performed at the Last Supper. The story would also have encouraged Christians to put their trust in God to provide for their every need.

2. The influence of the Old Testament is again apparent in this incident. In the book of Exodus we read how God provided food for the Israelites in the wilderness after they had escaped from Egypt. The prophet Elisha also performed a miracle similar to the one Mark tells (see 2 Kings 4:42–44). These stories would have been familiar to Mark and, no doubt, when he wrote about the feeding of the five thousand, he wanted his readers to see that Jesus was following in the tradition of the Old Testament. It was yet another way of saying that Jesus was the Messiah.

3. A popular image which Jews had of the future life was that of a banquet in heaven. The Messiah would act as host and those sharing the meal would be the saved. Perhaps Mark also had this in mind when writing his account of this miracle.

(iii) Jesus walks on the water 6:45–52

1. Mark deliberately sets the scene for this incident by separating Jesus (who stays to send away the crowd and to pray) from the disciples (who set out to cross the lake by boat).

2. Verse 52 suggests that Mark intended a connection between this miracle and the feeding of the five thousand which immediately precedes it. He emphasises total lack of understanding on the part of the disciples who are terrified and dumbfounded and whose 'minds were closed' (that is, they are blind to the truth).

3. The disciples do not understand the connection which Mark intends his readers to make. Again it is the Old Testament Mark has in mind. He wants to show how Jesus shares God's power over the sea. In the Old Testament God is said to have power to walk through or on the waves (for an example, see Job 9:8). (See also the comments on the stilling of the storm.)

100

4. This story is also presented as a rescue operation, though the disciples do not appear to be in any danger. Perhaps Mark saw the whole incident as having particular significance for his community. The following lessons could be learnt: that even if things go against you (there was a headwind) and progress is difficult and slow (the disciples were labouring at the oars), even if you feel abandoned by God (Jesus had sent his disciples from him while he stayed on land), or doubt that he is real (the disciples thought Jesus was a ghost), God still watches over you (Jesus saw that his disciples were in trouble v.48) and will come to save you at any time (Jesus caused the wind to cease in the middle of the night – the fourth watch (R.S.V.) was about 3 a.m.). Mark's readers could be assured of God's presence even in the darkest hour.

(iv) The feeding of the four thousand 8:1–10

1. It is usually suggested that this incident is an alternative version of the feeding of the five thousand. For this reason the comments made on the earlier miracle also apply to this one.

2. Mark intentionally used both stories to fit in with the overall plan of his gospel. It may be that he also wanted to suggest to his readers that Jesus' message was as much for Gentiles as Jews. The feeding of the five thousand is given a Jewish setting whereas it may be assumed that the feeding of the four thousand happened in Gentile territory (the Decapolis or Ten Towns is the location suggested by 7:31).

3. There may also be some symbolism intended in the numbers used in both feeding stories. If so, Mark was emphasising Jesus' ability to feed spiritually both Jew and Gentile. In the feeding of the five thousand the five loaves may represent the five law books of the Old Testament known as the Torah, and the twelve baskets left over may represent the twelve tribes of Israel. This was truly a Jewish feeding. In the feeding of the four thousand the seven loaves and the seven baskets left over may represent the seventy nations into which the Gentile world was traditionally divided. This would emphasise Jesus' ability to meet the needs of the whole world.

(v) The cursing of the fig tree 11:12–14, 20–25

1. This is perhaps the most difficult of all the miracles to understand because it is a miracle of destruction. Jesus acts completely out of character, and his behaviour is unreasonable; Mark tells us 'it was not the season for figs' (v.13).

2. Verses 22–25 suggest that Mark was using this to introduce teaching about faith and prayer, though, it must be admitted, there hardly seems to be any connection at all. Cursing a tree is hardly a good example of faith, prayer, or the forgiving spirit spoken of in verse 25!

3. What then is the interpretation? It could be that the story was originally a parable (see chapter 12). Mark placed it here because he wanted to give an example of what was going to happen to the Jews. They were like the fig tree – full of pretence. They boasted about their nation and their religion but really it was empty talk. When the Messiah came he was not received. Condemnation would follow as a result of their unfruitfulness, just as happened to the fig tree. Perhaps Mark felt it would paint a much more vivid picture if Jesus actually cursed a tree rather than told a story about one. He also chose to place the incident in the context of the rottenness of Jewish religion (at 11:15–19 Jesus has to clear the temple of the traders and money-changers), and in the build up to chapter 13 which prophesies the destruction of Jerusalem.

Questions on the nature miracles

1. 4:35–41
   (a) What beliefs did the Jews hold about the sea?
   (b) What is the difference between the attitude of Jesus and the attitude of the disciples when the storm threatens?
   (c) Why might this story have particular meaning for Mark's community?

2. 6:30–44
   (a) What, in this incident, reminds you of the Last Supper? (Look up 14:22–25.)

(b) How did the Old Testament influence the way Mark told this story?

3. 6:45–52
   (a) How does Mark set the scene for this story?
   (b) How did the disciples react when they saw Jesus walking on the water?
   (c) What significance might this story have had for Mark's community? (See note 4.)

4. 8:1–10
   (a) List the similarities, and the differences between this story and the account of the feeding of the five thousand.
   (b) Why might this story have been important in missionary work among Gentiles?

5. 11:12–14, 20–25
   (a) If this recounts a miracle performed by Jesus it seems totally out of character. Would you agree? Explain your answer.
   (b) How might this story be interpreted? (Read note 3 carefully before attempting an answer.)

Additional essay questions on the miracles

1. Recount two miracle stories in which an apparently dead person is raised. What symbolic significance might these miracles have?

2. Give (a) an example of a miracle where the faith of the sick person leads to a cure, and (b) an example of a miracle where the faith of someone else produces the same result.

3. How might the miracle stories have given comfort and strength to Mark's community?

4. How does Mark use some of the miracle stories to contrast Jesus' attitude with that of the Pharisees?

5. How might first century AD beliefs in magic have influenced the way Mark tells some of the miracle stories?

11.   The teaching of Jesus

a. Jesus the teacher

Mark makes it clear that from the very beginning of his ministry Jesus' main purpose was to *teach*. Jesus entered Galilee preaching (1:14–15), and when he arrived at Capernaum he went immediately to the synagogue and taught (1:21).

This pattern is continued throughout the gospel. Mark frequently depicts Jesus teaching the crowds who followed him, or speaks of him teaching in the towns he visited. In Mark, more than in any other gospel, people address Jesus by the title 'Teacher' (for example, at 9:5 Peter calls Jesus 'Rabbi', a word which means 'Teacher' or 'Master').

In fact, Mark presents Jesus very much in the style of the Jewish rabbi of his day. The rabbis were the teachers of Jewish scripture and they had the right to give judgment when disputes arose concerning the Law. They also gathered round them bands of pupils known as disciples. The disciples would sit at the feet of the rabbi, receiving his instruction and being under his authority. Much of the teaching given by the rabbis arose out of conversation or argument, and they frequently used parables to illustrate a point. Their source of authority was the Old Testament.

When we look at Jesus' method of teaching, we can see the similarities. Jesus selected a number of people to be his disciples, he gave them instruction and they were under his authority. Much of his teaching arose out of conversation or argument and he used parables as part of his method. The people recognised that Jesus taught with authority. He also used the Old Testament to support much of what he said and did.

With all this in mind, it will come as something of a surprise now to discover that really Mark gives us very little detail of Jesus' teaching. Rarely does he tell us *what* Jesus actually taught. Only to the disciples is any real teaching given, and then it seems they fail to understand what Jesus tells them.

b. Mark and 'the teaching'

It is highly unlikely that the teaching Mark includes in his gospel is all that he knew. Presumably he selected from a wider stock of material that particular teaching which served his purpose in writing. We already know from previous chapters something of what that purpose was. It was certainly not his aim to record absolutely everything he knew about Jesus. He was much more concerned to make the good news about him relevant to his own church, and to show them how Jesus' life had been beset by the same sort of problems that were troubling them. So Mark placed in his gospel only those bits of teaching which related directly to the situation of his readers. This means that we do not get an overall picture of Jesus' teaching from Mark, only some isolated sayings, a few parables, some conversations, usually with opponents, and explanations given to the disciples.

We must also accept that Mark has probably *adapted* the teaching he has used to suit his own purpose. What we are in fact dealing with is Mark's *interpretation* of the teaching of Jesus. This means that we cannot say with any degree of certainty that any of the so-called words of Jesus were actually spoken by him. (The situation becomes even more complicated when we remember that Mark did not get his information straight from Jesus' lips anyway. It came to him through the early church and it seems likely that it too had also adapted the message to suit its own needs.) No doubt the teaching reflects the spirit of Jesus' message but we have no cast-iron guarantee that these were his actual words.

It is crucial to our study that we bear in mind all that we have so far learned of Mark and his situation because, clearly, this had great influence on him as he wrote.

c. The parables

Before we look at some of the important themes of Jesus' teaching in Mark, it is necessary to say something about parables and Mark's understanding of them.

We generally assume that parables are colourful stories designed to illustrate Jesus' teaching and make it easier to understand and remember. It therefore comes as something of a shock to find out that this is *not* Mark's view of parables at all. Mark seemed to think that Jesus used parables to *prevent* people understanding his message! A strange idea, but one which, as we shall see, probably came about as a result of the persecution Mark's church was suffering.

The word 'parable' simply means the placing of one thing alongside another in order to compare or illustrate. There are some examples of parables in the Old Testament and, later on, the rabbis frequently used parables in their teaching. So when Jesus used parables he was using a form of teaching common in the east. It seems likely that the parables Jesus told were designed to do just what we imagine parables to do, namely to make the teaching clearer and more memorable. So why did Mark make things difficult?

We have seen in previous chapters how and why the idea of *secrecy and revelation* is important to Mark. The same reasons apply to his presentation of the parables. One thing it was not safe to do in the place where Mark lived was openly to declare your faith. To have done so would have meant almost certain persecution and probably death. However much you might have felt the urge to preach the gospel and make clear to everyone the message of Jesus, it simply was not safe to do so. The message had to be kept a secret and its true meaning revealed only to the few faithful Christians.

When Mark retold the parables of Jesus, he felt it necessary to show his readers how, even in Jesus' own life-time, the gospel message had been kept a secret from the majority of people (see 4:10–12). He presents the parables as though they were riddles. All those present hear the story but, because some do not have the key to the riddle, they are unable to understand.

Just as Mark's persecutors must have known the story of Jesus but failed to see its significance, so Jesus' hearers listen to the parables but fail to understand what they are about. Only the disciples are given the full meaning of the parables. In a similar way, it is only Mark's church members who know what the real significance of Jesus is to the world.

Three other reasons may also help us to see why Mark treated the parables in this way.

1. The early Christians were anxious to preserve, wherever possible, what was remembered of Jesus' teaching. As time went on, though some of the stories Jesus told were still remembered, the actual *context* in which they were spoken was forgotten. This meant that by the time the gospel writer came to write, the real meaning of the teaching was not entirely clear, and so he came to the view that Jesus taught in this way to conceal rather than reveal the truth . (See additional note at the end of this chapter.)

2. The early church developed the habit of treating the parables as *allegories*. An allegory is a story in code form which uses a number of symbols to stand in place of what it is really talking about (for example, in the interpretation to the parable of the sower, the seed is a symbol for the word). Each point in the story has to be interpreted and to do this you need to know the code, that is, to know what the symbols used mean. In an allegory you need continually to ask, 'What does *that* stand for?'

3. The early Christians believed that God *chose* to reveal his message to some (those who would be saved), and deliberately chose to keep it a secret from others (those who would not be saved). This idea was originally a Jewish one which Christians took over and used to explain why it was that so many people ignored the Christian message. Mark assumed that parables were used because they concealed the truth from those who were not meant to have it ('. . . but to those outside everything comes by way of parables, so that (as Scripture says) they may look and look, but see nothing; they may hear and hear, but understand nothing' 4:11–12). Those inside the church could easily have the parables explained to them, just as Jesus gave explanations to the disciples ('To you the secret of the kingdom of God has been given' 4:11).

d. Additional note

It is likely that the same parables were used to teach different things in the early church. For example, one preacher might have used the parable of the seed growing secretly (4:26–29) to teach about *patience*. The farmer sowed the seed and then could do nothing but wait patiently for nature to take its course. Another preacher might have used the same parable to emphasise the *activity* of God. Like the farmer at harvest, God would work quickly when it was time to bring in his kingdom.

If each teacher simply took the parables and adapted them to his needs, then it becomes almost impossible to be certain of the original meaning. All we can really do is to examine the way in which the gospel writer used them.

We can summarise as follows:–

1. Jesus taught in parables.
2. The early church preserved the parables but often lost the context in which they had been spoken. This meant that they were probably used in different ways.
3. The gospel writer chose to use the parables in a way that suited his own interests.

Questions for chapter 11

1. How does Mark emphasise that Jesus' main purpose was to be a teacher?

2. What does the word 'rabbi' mean? Write *five* lines on rabbis.

3. What similarities are there between Jesus and the rabbis?

4. What did Mark think was the purpose of parables? How does his view differ from the normally accepted one?

5. Why is it difficult to be certain that the words of Jesus in the gospel were actually spoken by him?

6. What is an allegory? Look up 4:1–20 and 12:1–12. Why are these parables really allegories?

12. Themes in Jesus' teaching

a. Theme 1: A new teaching

References

1:21–22   7:1–23
2:15–17   10:1–12
2:18–20   12:28–34
6:1–6

(i) Something different

At 1:27 Mark tells us that the people in the synagogue at Capernaum recognised what Jesus said and did as *a new kind of teaching*. Though these same people did not realise that Jesus was the Messiah, they did see that there was something special about him which made him stand out against their own religious leaders. For one thing, he taught with authority which distinguished him from the doctors of the law (or scribes) who tended simply to repeat the opinions of scribes who had gone before them, and would rarely give an opinion of their own. Jesus' teaching also involved taking positive action; doing good to others wherever the need existed. In the incident at Capernaum he healed the man possessed by an unclean spirit.

Similarly, when Jesus taught in the synagogue of his home town, the people recognised his powerful teaching and his ability to work miracles, even though they were offended by him.

Throughout Mark's gospel, we find that the reaction of the people to Jesus is one of astonishment and amazement at his words and works.

(ii) The old way

This *new teaching* brought Jesus into considerable trouble with the religious leaders of his day. In particular the Pharisees and Jesus are constantly at odds in Mark as you will remember from your study of the chapter on conflict.

The Pharisees believed that when they had proved to God that they could keep his laws faultlessly he would send the Messiah to save them. To try to ensure that the Law was never broken, they developed many more rules to safeguard the individual laws (these are known as the 'Tradition', e.g. 7:8 'the tradition of men'). Then they attempted to live by all of these rules.

(iii) Jesus and his critics

The Pharisees were critical of Jesus because it seemed to them that he was ignoring the Law and the Tradition. They found him sharing a meal with some of the outcasts of Jewish society, the tax-collectors and so-called sinners (2:15–17). They found his disciples ignoring the valued religious practice of fasting (2:18–20), and failing to conform to ancient Jewish tradition by ritually washing themselves before eating (7:1–23). The Pharisees were bound to suspect Jesus' motives. If Jesus were a real religious teacher in the tradition of the Old Testament, he would not behave like this!

(iv) The new way

Of course Mark wants us to see how blind the Pharisees were to what was happening. They continually failed to recognise that Jesus was the Messiah and, because of this, they failed to take account of the completely *new situation* which the Messiah had authority to bring in. This new situation meant that the Jews must adopt a whole new outlook on life. They must not allow themselves to be burdened with rules that they could not possibly keep. This new teaching of Jesus aimed to release people from the responsibility of obeying laws so that they could be free to think clearly about their relationship with God and with their fellowmen. To do good to others, for example, was a far better thing than obeying a law.

By word and example we find Jesus in Mark challenging the Pharisees' ideas. He eats with the outcasts despite the Old Testament rule that good people should not mix with the bad. He ignores much of the Tradition because it binds people to practices which in themselves become more important than dealing with human need where they see it. On the matter of divorce (10:1–12 see page 123 for further comment) he is not afraid to challenge the generally accepted interpretation of the Law or indeed, it seems, to challenge the Law itself. No rabbi would have done that. It would have been considered blasphemous. But Mark makes it clear that Jesus is more than a rabbi, he is the Messiah. As such he is bringing in a new, even more demanding teaching for a new age. The gospel message was that the kingdom of God was coming. For that, high moral standards would be required.

(v) The commandments of Jesus

When asked by a lawyer, 'Which commandment is first of all?' (12:28–34), Jesus summarised the Law into two commandments, (1) to love God with all your heart; (2) to love your neighbour as yourself. The combination of these two Old Testament rules is at the heart of Christian teaching. Together they provide a guiding principle on which human action can be based. There is then no question of people being forced strictly to follow a set of laws as the Pharisees were so keen to do.

Questions on Theme 1

1. How did Jesus' method of teaching differ from that of the lawyers?

2. How would you describe Jesus' attitude towards the outcasts of Jewish society?

3. What do you think Jesus meant when he said, 'It is not the healthy that need a doctor, but the sick; I did not come to invite virtuous people, but sinners'?

4. (a) What reply did Jesus give to those who criticised his disciples for not fasting?
   (b) What was the *meaning* of Jesus' reply?

5. (a) What was the reaction of the people when Jesus spoke in the synagogue of his home town?
   (b) How many brothers did Jesus have, according to Mark?

6. (a) What did Jesus teach concerning divorce?

111

(b) How did the teaching of Jesus on divorce differ from that of the rabbis? (See page 123 for comment.)

7. (a) 'Which commandment is first of all?' What did Jesus reply to this question?
   (b) How did the lawyer react to Jesus' answer?

b. Theme 2: Old and new

References

2:21–22	7:14–23
6:1–6	12:1–12

(i) Judaism or Christianity?

A constant problem which exercised the minds of the early Christians was how this new teaching of Jesus related to the old teaching and practices of Judaism. After all, the first Christians were Jews who had been brought up in the Jewish faith and were used to all the ritual that went with it – old habits die hard! The situation was made more complicated by the fact that during the first few years after Jesus' death, Christians had continued to attend the synagogue and worship alongside the Jews who did not accept that Jesus was the Messiah. As time went on, it became increasingly difficult for the two groups to continue together because of their differing views about Jesus. Eventually the Christians broke away to form a new religion.

Was it right that the Christians should break away from Judaism? Was this what Jesus wanted? Mark told two short parables to assure his readers that Jesus himself had foreseen this. At 2:21–22 we read about new and old cloth and new and old wine. It seems the point is this: just as a new piece of cloth which has not shrunk and is much stronger than the cloth surrounding it, will pull away from the old cloth; and just as old leather wineskins, brittle and already stretched, would burst when filled with new fermenting wine, so the old religion of Judaism with its own set teachings and practices could not contain the new teaching of Christianity.

(ii) Do the old rules still apply?

Even if Christianity was a new religion, the early Christians were still not sure whether they should give up all the rules of the old faith. After all, had not Jesus himself been faithful to the Old Testament and critical of those who neglected the Law (7:8)?

The Jews had very strict rules about food, and the Old Testament specified quite clearly what they were allowed to eat and what they were not allowed to eat. One question then, which was of real concern to the Christians was, 'Were they making themselves unclean by eating food forbidden by Jewish Law?' Mark wants to make quite clear to his readers that they have been set free from the old way of life. At 7:14–23 it seems that the real matter in Mark's mind is one to do with food (the question of the Pharisees at verse 5 was to do with ritual cleanliness rather than hygiene, and no mention is made of forbidden foods).

Jesus tells a parable which it appears nobody understands, even the disciples are '. . . as dull as the rest'. He explains that anything a person eats is a matter for the digestive system and not the heart. Therefore, things which enter the body from the outside (such as food) do not make people evil. Whereas from the heart (that is, from inside the person and nothing to do with food) come all sorts of evil thoughts, words and deeds, and it is these which 'defile' people. In other words, the sort of person you are will be apparent from your words and actions and what you eat will not affect that in any way. At verse 20 Mark spells it out for his readers, 'Thus he (Jesus) declared all foods clean.'

Mark is here very much concerned with the relationship between the old order (Judaism) and the new order (Christianity) and the way in which the new order was working out its own identity. Christianity was in the process of abandoning much of the ritual of Judaism and was concerning itself with the way people lead their lives (as the list at 7:21–23 makes clear).

(iii) The gospel spreads among Gentiles

By and large, Christianity spread more rapidly among Gentiles than it did among Jews. This puzzled the early Christians. After all, Jesus was a Jew who had been brought up

113

in that faith. Indeed, the Christians believed that Jesus was the *Jewish* Messiah – the one God had promised his people (Israel).

Why then had the Jews rejected Jesus? In telling of the incident when Jesus was rejected by the people of his home town (6:1–6) and in the parable of the vineyard (12:1–12), Mark shows how it was that Jesus' own countrymen chose to reject him. The people of Nazareth had the opportunity to hear what Jesus had to say and to see the miracles he performed, but they chose to ignore the signs, and because of this the gospel was given to others (Gentiles).

The parable (or, more correctly, allegory) of the vineyard gives us an insight into Mark's view of history. It first describes the situation the Jews were in before Jesus arrived on the scene. They had decided to lead their own lives and when God (the owner) sent the various prophets (the servants) to warn them about their bad behaviour, the Jewish authorities (the tenants) were hostile towards them. Eventually the Messiah (the son) was sent and he too was totally rejected. Verse 9 is about the *new situation*. The vineyard is given to others (the Gentiles). And, to reinforce that Christianity is a new religion in its own right, Mark quotes Psalm 118:22–23 (see vv. 10–11). Jesus is the cornerstone on which Christianity has been built.

Questions on Theme 2

1. What was Mark trying to teach his readers through the parables of the new and old wine and the new and old cloth?

2. What did Jesus mean when he said, 'nothing that goes into a man from outside can defile him; no, it is the things that come out of him that defile a man'?

3. Why was Mark anxious to show his readers that Jesus 'declared all foods clean'?

4. (a) In the parable of the vineyard, what do the following stand for: the vineyard; the owner; the tenants; the servants; the son?
   (b) What did Jesus mean when he described himself as a 'cornerstone'?

114

(c) How did the enemies of Jesus react to this story?

c. Theme 3: Discipleship

References

3:31–35	10:13–16	12:1–12
4:1–20	10:17–31	12:41–44
6:1–6	10:42–45	13:9–13

(i) The cost of discipleship

To be a member of the community Mark was writing for took some courage. Read 13:9–13. The things Mark speaks of here were actually happening to the members of his church. How could Mark help them in what he had to say about Jesus? This was undoubtedly what occupied his mind. What *could* you say to people who were being taken to court for their beliefs and made to explain themselves publicly, who were being beaten and generally hated for their faith? What *could* you say to people who were suffering family rifts which sometimes led to betrayals? You could warn them to be on their guard (v.9). You could offer them hope ('the man who holds out to the end will be saved' v.13). But that in itself was not enough. Mark wanted also to show them that the things they were now suffering were the same things that Jesus himself had suffered in his lifetime. Their present experiences had been Jesus' experiences when he was on earth. A number of incidents which Mark relates help to make this clear.

1. The parable of the vineyard (12:1–12) is about the way in which the Jewish authorities rejected Jesus. Mark's community were being similarly rejected by the Roman authorities.

2. When Jesus went to his home town he was rejected by the people there (6:1–6). The members of Mark's community were living in a situation where people were hostile to them, perhaps even people they had known all their lives who were offended at the message of Christianity.

3. In the incident related at 3:31–35 where Jesus' mother and brothers arrive to see him, Mark explains to his readers

115

how even members of Jesus' own family misunderstood what he was doing. At 3:21 Mark says that his family had '. . . set out to take charge of him; for people were saying that he was out of his mind.' Does Mark want us to think that they too have mistaken the Son of God for a madman? Those among Mark's Christian community who had been misunderstood or betrayed by members of their own family knew the pain that that brought. What could be worse? Here Mark offers them the comfort of knowing that Jesus also had been misunderstood and, in that sense, betrayed by his own family.

(ii) The qualities of a disciple

Courage and determination are two qualities which immediately come to mind in the light of what has just been said. The parable of the sower (4:1–20) shows that determination is a necessary quality of the disciple. It explains how various types of people react differently to the message of Christianity. These people, it seems, fall into two main categories – those who hear the Christian message but for various reasons are unable to make it the basis of their lives; and those who become true followers of Christ (those 'who bear fruit' v. 20). Mark makes it clear that those who fail to make the grade have not been *determined* enough. They have in some way or other given in to evil, either as a direct result of Satan's activity (v. 15), or through persecution (v. 17), or interest in wealth (v. 19). These are the people who 'look and look but see nothing', who 'hear and hear, but understand nothing' (v. 12).

(iii) The disciple must make sacrifices

1. We have already seen some of the sacrifices the disciple must be prepared to make. He may be called upon to cut himself off from family and friends. He may suffer hatred or be physically beaten.

Jesus' disciples had given up everything to be followers of Jesus (10:28) and now it was the turn of the members of Mark's church to make their sacrifices. What were the limits to which the disciple was expected to go in making his sacrifice? Mark had no doubts. It may even involve giving up one's life! Jesus did that very thing and so it was not too much to ask the disciple to do the same.

116

In a short incident at 12:41–44, Jesus is depicted watching people contribute towards the temple up-keep. The rich were giving only what they could easily afford. A poor widow came along and, though her contribution was very small, it represented all the money she had to live on – in other words, she had given away her life. Mark's church was well aware that Christianity demanded total giving, not just in terms of money but possibly even one's life.

2. In telling the story of the rich man at 10:17–31, Mark explains how some people, though attracted to the idea of becoming disciples, are not prepared to make the sacrifice. When Jesus told the man it was necessary for him to give up his wealth in order to be a true follower, it was more than he could face – the cost of discipleship was too great. The man had come to rely on his wealth for security and Jesus wanted him to see that to be a follower of his meant putting all your *trust* in God and relying on him as the sole source of security.

Trust is probably what is at the heart of 10:15, when Jesus says that those who do not accept the kingdom of God like a child will never enter it. The child provides an example of someone who relies entirely on others (his family) and accepts what is provided for him. In a similar way, the true disciple must be prepared to rely entirely on God for his well-being.

(iv) The true disciple and the life of service

The true disciple is simply one who does the will of God. Whoever does the will of God is counted a member of God's family (see 3:31–35).

The disciple must also be prepared to lead a life of service, as 10:42–45 makes clear. In this passage the traditionally accepted roles of master and servant are reversed. Those who are going to be the leaders of the Christian church must be prepared to follow the example of Jesus who came as a servant.

Questions on Theme 3

1. How does Mark use the incident of a visit from Jesus' mother and brothers to teach about true family relationships?

2. 'A prophet will always be held in honour except in his home town.' What do you understand this saying to mean?

3. Why might the story of Jesus' rejection at Nazareth have had special significance for the members of Mark's church?

4. What do you understand to be the meaning of the parable of the sower?

5. (a) Describe the conversation between Jesus and the stranger at 10:17–22.
   (b) What prevented the man from following Jesus' advice?

6. How would you summarise Jesus' teaching about wealth?

7. In the incident at 12:41–44, why was the very small gift of the woman so significant?

8. What special significance might 13:9–13 have had for the members of Mark's community?

d. Theme 4: The coming of the kingdom of God

References

4:26–29
4:30–34

What did Mark understand by the term 'the kingdom of God'? In some places in his gospel it seems that the kingdom of God had already come in Jesus (e.g. 1:15). Where Jesus was, there was the kingdom of God. At other times, it seems that the kingdom of God was still to come (e.g. 9:1). Mark recounts two of Jesus' parables which help to explain what the kingdom of God is like (the parable of the seed growing secretly 4:26–29, and the parable of the mustard seed 4:30–34). The kingdom is, it seems, both present

118

and future. It has come in Jesus but still has to develop into full maturity.

The parable of the seed growing secretly emphasises the lack of control man has over the process of nature. The farmer sows the seed and then continues his normal daily routine. The seed grows, though the farmer does not know how. It is the ground which produces the crop, not the farmer. His efforts are only needed again at harvest time.

Mark probably understood the parable to mean that followers of Jesus must be like the farmer. They must wait patiently for God to bring in his kingdom, even though they might not at present be able to see a development towards this. The seed has already been sown in Jesus. No doubt the members of Mark's persecuted church must have frequently felt impatient and discouraged, and wondered if God was really taking any action. This parable urged them to put their trust in God just as the farmer put his trust in the soil. Soon God's kingdom would come (harvest time in the parable) and then they would be given their reward.

The main point of the parable of the mustard seed is to contrast the smallness of the seed with the greatness of the shrub. What seems an insignificant beginning (the ministry of Jesus which was largely rejected, followed by the lack of progress in Mark's own church) can develop into something spectacular and enormous (the kingdom of God). Again, Mark's readers could find encouragement here, and could perhaps identify with the birds who found shelter in the branches of the tree.

Questions on Theme 4

1. What does the parable of the seed growing secretly teach about *patience*?

2. What special word of encouragement does the parable of the seed growing secretly offer the persecuted Christian?

3. Why might the parable of the mustard seed be called a parable of contrast?

119

e. Theme 5: Teaching about the future

Reference

13:1–37

(i) Background information

What was God's plan for the future and how would the faithful disciple know when the kingdom of God would finally come?

In chapter 13 of his gospel, Mark deals with these issues. He combines past, present and future to give his readers an insight into God's plans. It is set in the form of a talk from Jesus to four disciples, and no doubt Mark was influenced in the way he wrote by two forms of literature current in his day.

1. Apocalyptic writings. The word 'apocalyptic' means a 'revelation' or an 'unveiling'. Apocalyptic books claim to reveal things which are normally hidden, or to reveal the future. The Old Testament book of Daniel is a good example of Jewish apocalyptic writing. Usually what inspired the writing of such literature was some disaster which had befallen the nation. The writer would attempt to show that, however bad things seemed, God was fully in control and would eventually settle things in a fair and just way. The aim was to give those already suffering, hope or assurance that the future would bring them deserved reward for their faithfulness.

2. The farewell discourse or sermon. It was thought to be the practice of great religious teachers to deliver a farewell sermon to their followers before they died. The Old Testament contains many such addresses from great leaders like Moses and David. Usually the talk would include a look back over the events of their lives and a look forward into the future and what it might hold for the nation. The great teacher would urge his followers to remain faithful whatever trouble or sufferings might come upon them.

(ii) Some familiar themes

Chapter 13 of Mark is a blend of these two forms of Jewish literature. It contains some apocalyptic material and, placed where it is immediately before Jesus' suffering and death, is like a farewell sermon. Familiar themes of Mark remain strong. Secrecy is an example. The sermon is delivered in private to Peter, James, John and Andrew. This is a clear indication that Mark sees it as part of the 'secret', knowledge of which is intended only for truly faithful followers. In any case, only those totally involved in the experiences of the early Christians would appreciate the significance of the sermon and understand its message.

The fight against evil is another familiar theme. Jesus' war with the demons and Satan, which has been waged throughout the gospel, will have to be continued by the church until the end of time, when a final battle will see their destruction.

(iii) The life of Jesus and the life of his church are one

It will have become clear by now that, as Mark wrote, he saw the life of Jesus and the life of his Christian community as one. He did not trouble to disentangle what he perhaps knew to be genuine teaching of Jesus from the direct issues which concerned the members of his church. His aim was to give comfort and assurance to his readers – comfort, to know that they were not experiencing anything which Jesus himself had not first experienced; assurance, that God had not forgotten them in their time of trouble, but that all things were working towards his final plan.

It is important to bear this in mind as you read chapter 13.

(iv) The sermon itself

The sermon begins with a prophecy of the destruction of the temple. Whether this was a genuine prophecy of Jesus or of Mark is impossible to say. At the time when Mark wrote, the temple was either in imminent danger of destruction (along with the rest of Jerusalem) or it had already been destroyed (in which case, Mark is recording *history* rather than prophecy). After an uprising of the Jews in AD 66, the Romans sent in a vast army and besieged Jerusalem. In AD 70 the whole city, including the temple, was destroyed.

It is likely that the difficult phrase at verse 14, 'But when you see "the abomination of desolation" usurping a place

121

which is not his (let the reader understand)', also refers to the destruction of Jerusalem. It is written in veiled language which suggests that it was probably not safe for Mark to put down what he really wanted to say. But he knew his readers would understand exactly what he meant.

The 'abomination of desolation' is a direct quotation from the book of Daniel where it refers to a pagan altar which was set up in the temple at Jerusalem by the Greek king, Antiochus Epiphanes, about 168 BC. This was a most terrible thing to the Jews and Mark obviously has something similarly distasteful in mind, probably the destruction of Jerusalem. If this is the case, then the one who 'usurps the place which is not his' would be the Roman Emperor who, for Mark, represents evil in human form (he is the anti-Christ). Not only is he the one responsible for destroying the holy city, Jerusalem, he is also the one responsible for the suffering of Mark's community.

Whatever the 'abomination of desolation' means, it is the signal that the last days have come and great suffering and distress is to follow. The disciple is told not to be alarmed by all this (wars, earthquakes, famines, great suffering) nor to be misled by people posing as the Messiah. The promise is given that the 'chosen' or the 'elect' will be saved (v. 13) and that the time of suffering will be cut short for their sake (v.20).

An insight is given (vv. 24–27) into what the end of the world will be like. Here Mark reproduces material from the apocalyptic writings of the Old Testament in order to convey a supernatural picture of the end. The promise remains that the Son of Man (here, a divine figure) will save the chosen, who will be gathered from all over the world.

Mark ends the chapter with a number of sayings and parables on the general theme of the need to be watchful in view of the coming end of the world. The faithful disciple must be constantly 'awake'!

Questions on Theme 5

1. What did Jesus forecast concerning the temple?

2. What question did Peter, James, John and Andrew ask Jesus? Did it receive a reply?

3. What do you think Mark meant by the coded statement, ' " the abomination of desolation" usurping a place which is not his (let the reader understand)'?

4. What warnings are given about the future?

5. What promise is given to 'the chosen'?

6. What lesson is to be learnt from the fig tree?

7. When did Mark think the end of the world would take place?

8. Why must the door-keeper stay awake?

The following additional material should also be studied

3:22–30
This has been fully dealt with in the chapter on miracles but note should be taken here of the two short parables, the kingdom divided against itself and the strong man's house.

4:21–25
Parables about the lamp and the measure.

9:38–50
The exorcist who was not a follower, and some sayings of Jesus.

11:12–14, 20–25
The fig tree has been dealt with in the chapter on miracles. Note in addition the teaching on faith, prayer and forgiveness.

Note on divorce

Deuteronomy 24:1–4 made it clear that divorce was lawful. If a man wished to divorce his wife (a woman could not divorce her husband) he had to write her a note of divorce (to show that she was free to re-marry). Grounds for divorce were not specified. Deuteronomy 24:1 is vague and says that a man may divorce his wife if '. . . she does not win his favour because he finds something shameful in her.' The teaching of the rabbis differed when they came to interpret this passage. Some said that it meant divorce was only allowed if the woman had been unfaithful to her husband.

Others thought it meant that a man could divorce his wife if she did no more than overcook his dinner.

Jesus pointed out that Moses only made such a law because of the weakness of human nature, and that the real will of God was made clear at the time of creation. Genesis 2:24 speaks of a man leaving his father and mother to become united with his wife, '. . . and the two become one flesh.' In other words, a permanent relationship is created, and as such divorce could not be allowed under any circumstances.

Additional essay questions on the teaching

1. How did the *new teaching* of Jesus differ from the *old teaching* of the Pharisees? Give some examples in your answer.

2. What were some of the problems which the early Christians faced as they broke away from Judaism?

3. The feeling of rejection was no doubt strong among the members of Mark's community. Give examples to show how Jesus himself was misunderstood and rejected by people during his lifetime.

4. How does Mark explain the kingdom of God to his readers?

5. What, according to Mark, did Jesus foretell would happen at the end of the world?

6. As Mark wrote, he saw the life of Jesus and the life of his Christian community as one. Discuss this statement giving examples from the gospel.

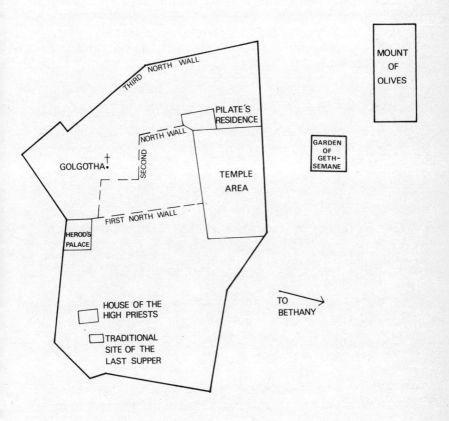

Plan of Jerusalem

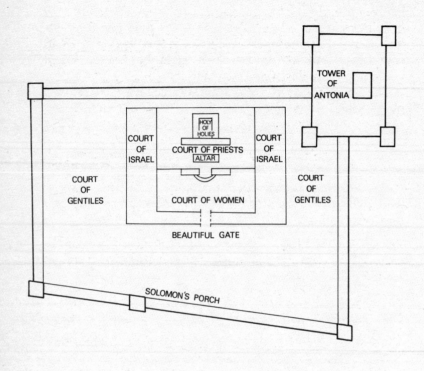

Plan of the temple at Jerusalem

Notes on the temple

The temple shown on the plan was the third to be built on the same site. Solomon had built the first temple and this was destroyed by the Babylonians in 586 BC. The second had been built after the Jews had returned from the Exile in Babylon about 520 BC. Herod the Great began the building of the third temple in 20 BC. Work was not finally completed until AD 63 just seven years before the temple was completely destroyed by the Romans.

The temple was a place for sacrifice. (It was the only place where Jews made sacrifice. There were many synagogues throughout the country where the Jews held their Sabbath day worship, but only one temple.) Animal sacrifices were made morning and evening each day by the priests.

The temple was also a place of pilgrimage – devout Jews were expected to visit the temple sometime during the great religious festivals.

The Holy of Holies – the innermost shrine of the temple, visited only once a year on the Day of Atonement by the High Priest.

The Court of Priests – altars were placed here, on which the priests made sacrifice.

The Court of Israel – only Jewish men were allowed to enter.

The Court of the Women – this was an area open to any Jew.

The Court of the Gentiles – this was open to anyone, Jew or Gentile. Gentiles were not allowed to go beyond this point into the temple itself. The penalty for doing so was death.

13. The Passion narrative

Chapters 14, 15, 16

a. The confirmation of the good news

The last three chapters of Mark are usually known as the 'Passion narrative'. The word 'passion' comes from the Latin *passio* meaning 'suffering'. The word 'narrative' is attached to it because this section of the gospel tells an uninterrupted story of Jesus' last hours and death. Up to this point Mark has either not known where or when events took place, or felt free to arrange them as he thought best. (See chapter 1 for an account of the gospel in the oral period.) When he came to this period of Jesus' life he had available to him an ordered account of events, including details of the time and place at which they occurred.

Why the story came to Mark as a whole is not difficult to explain. The death of Jesus and his resurrection are the central part of the Christian faith. Jesus had taught that if you followed him, suffered and died, then you would rise again. This is what happened to Jesus. It confirmed the good news.

When the early church went to proclaim the gospel, it preached the news of Christ crucified and risen. This was the foundation of its faith. The events surrounding this one great event were told and retold countless times, and a detailed account passed on to each new convert. Everyone knew the story and it was probably the earliest part of the good news to be written down.

Mark included this narrative in his gospel in much the same form as it came to him. There was no need for him to try to imagine the order of events since, from the earliest days of the church, they had been assembled and preserved. However, this did not stop him inserting details, when he thought necessary, and drawing together in the Passion narrative all the main themes which had interested him throughout his gospel.

We find the prophecies of the Old Testament still being fulfilled, as are those Jesus has made about himself, the Son of Man. Conflict, the guilt of the Jewish authorities, the innocence and suffering of Jesus, all reach their climax in the trial and crucifixion. Finally, the themes of the disciples and the church are bound even more closely together in the description of the Last Supper, and by the message from Jesus with which Mark ends his gospel.

b. The importance of Jerusalem

Jerusalem was the centre of Judaism. The temple, which the Jews regarded as God's dwelling-place on earth, was there and, according to scripture, God himself had chosen the city as the site for it.

The original temple had been built by King Solomon in obedience to God's words to his father, David (2 Sam. 7). The temple of Jesus' time was the third one to have been built. Herod the Great began work on it in 20 BC, and although the section used for worship was complete, the surrounding buildings were not finished until AD 63.

The temple was the only place where the Jews could offer sacrifice and as such was a place of pilgrimage. Pilgrims came not only from Palestine but from all over the known world, wherever Jews had settled. In Deuteronomy 16 God commanded that his people should come into his presence three times a year at the place which he would choose as a dwelling. Jews understood this to mean the temple in Jerusalem, and at the festivals of Passover, Weeks and Tabernacles the city was packed with pilgrims.

Jerusalem came to represent the nation. Devotion to the temple and its sacrifices, as well as the Law of Moses, had united the Jews at times of persecution. Their obedience to the Law and the belief that they were God's chosen people had kept them separate from the Gentiles. In Old Testament times, when the Jews strayed from the Law, the prophets had reminded them of their duty to God and warned them of the terrible consequences of ignoring it. Jesus was in many ways like an Old Testament prophet calling people to observe God's laws and so save themselves from destruction.

Jerusalem was the city where, it was believed, the Messiah would be proclaimed king and where he would reign. A passage in Zechariah (9:9) tells of the coming of Jerusalem's king, 'Your king is coming to you, his cause won, his victory gained, humble and mounted on an ass, on a foal . . . '

Mark describes Jesus' entry into Jerusalem in similar terms (11:1–10). The people cry 'Hosanna!' which means 'O save us!' The thought is perhaps of one come to save them from the Romans. But the procession Jesus leads goes straight to the temple indicating that he has come to bring a different sort of salvation. It was thought that God would send the Messiah at the time of the Passover and Jesus chose this festival to make his entry when the city was overflowing with pilgrims.

Jesus came as the Messiah to fulfil Old Testament prophecy. He had to go to Jerusalem, the centre of national and religious life, to call God's people to repentance even though he realised that it would cost him his life.

When Christians looked back to the events of the Passion they saw Jesus rejected by the Jews and the old covenant, or agreement, between the Jews and God brought to an end. The tearing of the curtain in the temple at the instant of Jesus' death probably symbolised this for them.

Christians believed that the temple had been replaced by the church. The word 'church' does not mean a building, in the way that the temple was a building, but refers to all the people who believed in Jesus. They were the 'church'. Those who followed Jesus were filled with God's Spirit, the Holy Spirit. So just as in the past God had dwelt in the temple, now he dwelt in his church – in each individual Christian who had been baptised with the Holy Spirit.

Since the blood of Jesus was the sign of the new covenant, the sacrifices in the temple were no longer necessary and, as far as Christians were concerned, the temple ceased to be of importance. In Christian belief Jerusalem became the place where the old covenant ended, the new began, and from which the gospel went out into the world.

c. The Last Supper 14:12–25

(i) New meaning for the bread and wine

According to Mark, the Last Supper was a Passover meal. He says that it took place on the day the lambs were being slaughtered, but traditionally this happened on the day before the Passover meal itself. It is likely that, as a Gentile, Mark did not know the details of the Jewish festival and made a mistake, but this is a minor point. What was important to him was the meaning of the Passover meal itself.

The Passover celebrated the escape of the Israelites from slavery in Egypt. It was believed that seven weeks after this they had assembled at Mount Sinai and made a covenant, or agreement, with God. This covenant was established by the blood of a sacrificial animal being flung over the people (Exod. 24:8). Witnessing the sacrifice and being marked by the blood was like signing a legal document, and the event confirmed that the Israelites were God's chosen people.

During the Last Supper Jesus behaved like the host in a Jewish house. He blessed the bread and the wine and handed them to his guests. But he gave these actions new meaning. The bread he broke represented his body and the wine his blood which was to be shed at the crucifixion.

Just as the Passover celebrated the escape from slavery in Egypt so, for Mark, the Last Supper celebrated the escape of man from slavery to the powers of evil. And just as the Israelites at Mount Sinai became part of the old covenant with God by having the blood of an animal flung over them, so now those who took part in the Last Supper and drank the wine became part of the new covenant.

(ii) The importance of the Last Supper to the church

The most important service the Christians of Mark's church celebrated was Communion. When they broke the bread and drank the wine they were imitating the actions of Jesus and the disciples at the Last Supper. They were also remembering Jesus' self-sacrifice on the cross when his blood was 'shed for many', which meant for them.

The sharing of the Communion meal was a sharing in the covenant Jesus had established, but it was also a sharing in his death. The Communion united Jesus with his followers, just as the ceremony of baptism did. For Christians this meant being willing to share in Jesus' death and resurrection.

To the Christian victims of persecution (see page 18) to drink the cup which Jesus drank really did mean to suffer as harshly as Jesus had suffered on the cross. The threat of a terrible death on account of their faith faced them constantly. They drew the spiritual strength they needed to live as Christians by taking the sacrament of the bread and wine at the Communion service.

When they succeeded in living in the way that Jesus had taught, serving each other, healing the sick, loving God and their neighbour, then they found that Jesus reigned amongst them.

They were the people of God of the new covenant, and their membership of it was symbolised by the re-enactment of the Last Supper in their Communion service.

d. Mark's portrayal of the death of Jesus 15:21–39

(i) Mark's brief account

The crucifixion is the cruel climax of Jesus' earthly life. We should expect a Christian account of such an important event to be filled with detail, but when we look at verses 21–39 we find that although it is detailed compared with many other incidents in the gospel it is still surprisingly brief.

Simon of Cyrene carries the cross to the place of execution, Jesus refuses drugged wine, he is fixed to the cross, his clothes are divided, two bandits are executed with him, he is mocked by his enemies, there is darkness, he cries to God and dies, the temple curtain is torn, and a centurion says he was a son of God.

One reason for the lack of detail is that Peter and the disciples had fled and Jesus was quite alone. So when Christians began to ask what had happened at the crucifixion an account of events had to be put together without the evidence of any close Christian eye-witnesses. The only ones mentioned are women who watched 'from a distance'.

Christians believed that Jesus had lived his life in complete obedience to God. It was as a result of this obedience that he had come into conflict with those evil men who

132

eventually killed him. Mark shows Jesus before his arrest, praying and asking God if he really had to suffer, and ending his prayer by saying, 'Yet not what I will, but what thou wilt' (14:36). Immediately after this Jesus is arrested. The answer to the prayer is clear; God requires obedience even if, in this sinful world, it means suffering and death.

The first Christians reasoned that if Jesus had died through obedience to God's will, then all that had happened must have been foreseen by God and written in the Old Testament. So to interpret what had happened at the crucifixion Christians turned to the Old Testament. There they searched for hints of what was to befall the Messiah and, by this means, an account of the crucifixion was put together by the church.

When Mark came to write his gospel he had the church's account of the crucifixion available to him. He used the words of the Old Testament as a way of demonstrating the Christian belief that events had followed the course which God had foreseen. At the same time Mark put in comments of his own to emphasise those points he thought to be important.

(ii) Mark's sources and the meaning of events

One important source of information was Psalm 22. Verse 18 says, 'They share out my garments among them and cast lots for my clothes.' Verse 7 says, 'All who see me jeer at me . . . and wag their heads.' Verse 1 says, 'My God, my God, why hast thou forsaken me?' If you compare these quotations with Mark 15:24, 29 and 34, you will see how Mark has made use of them.

What he is saying is simply that the crucifixion was foreseen by God. For Mark, all the incidents which make up his account of the crucifixion are filled with meaning.

15:26 Jesus was executed on the charge of being 'The King of the Jews'. He was innocent of claiming this title in a political sense, though, as the Messiah, he was king in a very real way. Mark's aim is to show that Jesus is innocent of the charge and that his execution is unjust.

15:29–32 Those who abuse Jesus represent the men of evil who have plotted against him from the start. They mock Jesus as the Messiah who can save others but not himself.

133

They accuse him again, as they did at his trial, of claiming that he will pull down the temple and rebuild it in three days.

The words sum up the opposition Jesus has suffered throughout his ministry. Mark puts them here as it is at this moment that evil appears triumphant. Satan has done his worst, now it is God who, with the resurrection, will demonstrate evil's complete defeat. This is the last we hear of opposition in the gospel.

15:33 The darkness which fell over the whole land is Mark's comment on the action of the Jewish authorities. The crucifixion of their promised Messiah was the most evil deed they could perform. Their whole land is in the grip of evil men and Mark expresses this idea symbolically by saying that it was in darkness.

15:34 The words which Jesus speaks come from Psalm 22:1. They are usually called the 'cry of dereliction', that is, the cry of one who felt abandoned by God.

But the words are not simply a cry of despair. They are the opening words of a psalm which is too long to quote in full. They point forward to the end of the psalm which is a hymn of praise to God. Man suffers, says the psalm, without understanding why. At times he appears abandoned by God, but all power and wisdom belong to God so, in spite of suffering, turn to him again and have faith. The mixture of despair and hope contained in Jesus' words summed up the feelings of the early Christians whose faith was tested to the limit by the threat of death.

15:38 Mark believed that at the moment of Jesus' death his earthly work was accomplished. The new covenant was made and the curtain in the temple torn from top to bottom is the symbol of the ending of the old covenant. God is no longer hidden in the temple. The barrier between man and God is removed. Now man can meet God in his own life if he is a member of the community which follows Jesus – the church. This community is to be the 'house of prayer for all the nations' (11:17).

15:39 Mark makes this clear by the comment of the centurion, 'Truly this man was a son of God.' These words from a Gentile hint at a church which will include people from all races.

e. Resurrection and mystery 15:40–16:8a

(i) The burial: 15:40–47

Mark begins his account of the burial of Jesus by using the same method that he used in describing the crucifixion. The women watching from a distance are an echo of Psalm 38:11, 'My friends and my companions shun me in my sickness, and my kinsfolk keep far away.'

The man who goes to Pilate to ask for Jesus' body is Joseph of Arimathaea, a member of the Sanhedrin. A Roman soldier has already called Jesus 'a son of God', now a Jew who 'looked forward to the kingdom of God' makes this gesture of faith. Mark seems to suggest that Jesus is already drawing together Gentiles and Jews.

It is possible that Joseph removed the body as an act of charity, or because the Old Testament (Deut. 21:23) ordered that a body should not be left out overnight. Whatever his reason, Joseph's act was a brave one since he associated himself with a man executed for a political offence. Mark would have seen more significance in the act than charity or obedience to the law.

He emphasises that Jesus was really dead. Pilate sends for the centurion to find out the time of death and then gives permission for the burial. Usually no care was taken with the bodies of those executed, and in other parts of the empire it was certainly Roman custom to leave them on display.

Mark also emphasises that there was no mistake on the women's part about the tomb in which Jesus was laid. No one would be able to say that the resurrection had not taken place, that they had returned to the wrong tomb. The women were watching and saw where he was laid. As there was no time before the Sabbath to anoint Jesus' body he was wrapped in a sheet (coffins were not used), laid in a tomb, and the entrance was sealed with a stone shaped like a wheel.

(ii) The Resurrection: 16:1–8a

The women returned to the tomb early on the Sunday morning with oils to anoint the body in the customary fashion. This was the third day, counting the day of the crucifixion and the Sunday itself. They discover that the tomb which was sealed is open and the body gone.

But there is a greater shock yet for the women. Sitting in the tomb is a youth dressed in white. Mark no doubt intends us to understand that the youth is an angel. Who but an angel would deliver divine messages? The women are dumbfounded, a reaction which confirms that they are in the presence of the divine.

The angel's message repeats what Jesus had prophesied, 'He has been raised again.' Then the angel delivers a message for the 'disciples and Peter: "He is going on before you into Galilee; there you will see him as he told you." ' This message was not only for those referred to but, in Mark's thinking, for the church also.

It again promises the fulfilment of one of Jesus' prophecies. At 14:28 Jesus says, 'after I am raised again I will go on before you into Galilee.' It refers to the mission of the church. The name 'Galilee' in the Old Testament meant the 'land of the heathen', and it seems likely that in this case Mark thought of it as referring to the Gentile world. The last message from Jesus then becomes a promise to his church that he will lead it out into the Gentile world.

The final sentences of the gospel (v. 8a) emphasise the terror of the women. Mark's intention is to tell his readers that the women had been brought face to face with divine activity, and that it was terrifying. All that had happened had been the result of God's action. This action now pointed to the future – to the life of the church for which Mark wrote.

(iii) Mystery

In every religion there is a point at which explanations fail. The resurrection of Jesus is such a point. We cannot supply a neat, scientific explanation for what occurred. One reason is that we do not have sufficient information. Another is that this is the point at which man's understanding fails.

With this event something happened to which we can only give the name 'mystery'.

If there were no such point of mystery then there would be no religion. To believe in Jesus requires faith. If everything could be explained in human terms no faith would be required and Christianity would not be a religion.

With his resurrection, Jesus' own faith in and obedience to God are shown to have been justified. He is not abandoned to the power of evil. Death was evil's ultimate weapon and is man's final enemy. Yet Jesus was freed from death's hold by God, and those who have faith in Jesus believe that they too will be freed.

How this can be accomplished only God knows. Faith means having confidence in someone without demanding that everything should be explained. Those who follow Jesus have such faith. Some things must remain a mystery. That is the nature of religion.

f. Mark's 'unsatisfactory' ending 16:8b–20

The gospel written by Mark comes to an abrupt end at 16:8a. Either one or more of Mark's readers felt this ending to be unsatisfactory and added his own. Even in the English translation it is clear that the second part of verse 8 is written by a different person – the language is not Mark's.

It is the same with verses 9–20. These seem to have been assembled from the other gospels and from the Acts of the Apostles, and they summarise stories about Jesus recorded in those books. You can compare the various accounts yourself.

Mark 16:9–11 : John 20:1–2
       12–13 : Luke 24:13–35
       15 : Matt. 28:19
       19 : Acts 1:9

It has been suggested that the end part of the gospel scroll was lost and that the missing section contained accounts of Jesus' appearances after his resurrection as the other gospels do.

If a part was lost it must have been very soon after the gospel was written as scholars believe that the copies used by Matthew and Luke in writing their gospels ended at verse

8. If the loss happened so early in the gospel's history we must explain why it was that Mark, or one of the members of his church, did not rewrite the missing portion.

Another suggestion for the sudden ending is that Mark may have been arrested or died at this point and therefore had been unable to finish his work. But it is almost unbelievable that he was forced to stop where he might freely have chosen to.

We have to bear in mind also that to end the book so abruptly would be quite out of keeping with other literature of that time. But Mark was an original writer and invented the form of literature we call a 'gospel', so perhaps he decided on a new type of ending as well.

But let us suppose that Mark chose to end his gospel at 16:8a. Can we suggest what his reason for such abruptness might have been? He leads up to it by showing the women coming to the tomb to anoint Jesus' body. Then, quite suddenly, they are faced by an open tomb, a youth (angel), and a message from Jesus whom they had thought dead.

What has happened? Jesus has been raised again – evil has been defeated. The greatest miracle of all confronts the women. They are terrified by this manifestation of God's power. They flee. What more can be said in the face of this tremendous mystery? Nothing, Mark seems to suggest. He lays down his stylus. The good news has been told.

Was Mark's ending unsatisfactory? Was part of the scroll lost? Was Mark unable to complete it? Or was this the terrifying, mysterious ending that Mark had planned? We do not know the answer, and it is up to every reader of Mark's gospel to supply his own.

Themes in the Passion narrative

1. The fulfilment of Old Testament prophecy
   14:21, 27 (see Zech. 13:7), 49; 15:24–36 (see section d. of this chapter), 40.

2. The fulfilment of Jesus' prophecy
   14:50, 66–72; 15:23; 16:6–7.

3. Further prophecy by Jesus
   14:8–9, 17–21, 25, 27–30, 62.

138

4. The conflict with evil
   14:1–2, 10–11, 41–46, 53; 15:22–37.

5. The failure of the disciples
   14:37–41, 50.

6. Jesus' teaching and purpose
   14:22–25.

7. Suffering as the result of obedience to God's will
   14:36, 65; 15:17–19, 24–39.

8. The innocence of Jesus
   14:55–56.

9. The guilt of the Jewish authorities
   14:55, 64; 15:1, 10.

10. The end of secrecy
    14:62.

11. The church
    14:22–25; 15:39; 16:7.

12. Prayer
    14:35–36.

Questions for chapter 13

1. 14:3–9
   (a) Describe the anointing of Jesus at Bethany.
   (b) What did Jesus mean by the words 'she is beforehand with anointing my body for burial'?
   (c) What memorial does Jesus say that the woman who anointed him will have?

2. 14:12–16
   (a) When did the Last Supper take place?
   (b) What arrangements were made to obtain a room for the meal?
   (c) What was the Passover?

3. 14:17–31
   (a) Who does Jesus prophesy will betray him?
   (b) Describe the words and actions of Jesus during the Last Supper.

(c) Describe the conversation which took place on the Mount of Olives.

4. 14:32–52
   (a) Which disciples did Jesus take with him when he prayed at Gethsemane?
   (b) Write out the prayer Jesus said.
   (c) Why did Jesus say, 'The spirit is willing, but the flesh is weak'?
   (d) Who betrayed Jesus and how?

5. 14:53–65
   (a) Where was the trial of Jesus before the Council held?
   (b) What was Jesus accused of saying?
   (c) Why did the High Priest tear his robes?
   (d) What was the judgment of the Council?

6. 14:66–72
   Describe what happened to Peter while Jesus was before the Council.

7. 15:1–20
   (a) What does Pilate ask Jesus and what does Jesus reply?
   (b) Why did Pilate ask the crowd what he should do with Jesus?
   (c) Why did the crowd give the answer it did?
   (d) Why was Barabbas released?
   (e) What did the Roman soldiers do to Jesus?

8. 15:21–39
   (a) Who carried the cross for Jesus?
   (b) What was the place of execution called?
   (c) Describe four incidents which occurred as Jesus was being crucified.
   (d) What words did Jesus cry out?
   (e) What did the Roman soldier say?

9. 15:40–47
   (a) Who were the women watching from a distance?
   (b) Who went to Pilate to ask for Jesus' body, and what did Pilate do?
   (c) What was done with Jesus' body?

10. 16:1–8a
    (a) Why did the women go to the tomb?
    (b) What did they discover?
    (c) What message was given to them and how did they react?

11. In what way does the Passion narrative differ from the earlier part of Mark's gospel? How do you account for this difference?

12. Explain the importance of Jerusalem and why Jesus went there.

13. Why is the Communion service so important to Christians?

14. How does Mark show that Jesus was innocent, and how does he place the guilt for Jesus' death more on the Jewish than the Roman authorities?

15. Mark's description of Jesus' death contains many Old Testament phrases. How do you account for this? Give two or three examples to illustrate your answer.

16. Explain the importance of the resurrection and of the youth's message for the church.

17. Do you think Mark originally ended his gospel at 16:8a?

14. 'Who do men say I am?'

Now that we have completed our study of Mark's gospel, what picture do you have of Jesus? Is it different from the one you had *before* you began this study? What picture do you have of Mark, and can you sense something of the situation his readers were experiencing? Do you feel you know more about Mark than you do about Jesus? In a way we hope you do because we have been studying Jesus through the eyes of Mark. What we have done, in fact, is to build up Mark's picture of Jesus – a sort of verbal identikit.

a. The problem of history

If we have been studying Mark's idea of Jesus, what about the real Jesus? What do we know about Jesus that is free from someone's interpretation of him? Can we uncover some pure historical facts about him?

Despite what history teachers might like you to believe, pure historical facts about anything are hard to come by. So-called 'historical facts' have always been *reported* or *recorded* by someone who in so doing, either deliberately or unconsciously, has placed his own interpretation on them. Even recent history suffers from this, let alone ancient history, where writers felt quite free to alter great chunks of past events to suit their purpose in writing. So, we have to be on our guard when we are dealing with history and must be prepared to say things like, 'such and such *probably* happened but we cannot be absolutely *certain* about it.'

b. The Jesus of history

When we come to look at Jesus we are in a similar position. As a character of ancient history, we have to admit that we cannot be absolutely certain about any of the events of his life – that is, if we want proof. It does, however, seem

142

highly probable that at least the main events of Jesus' life happened as the gospel writers tell us. But, in a sense, we have to accept even that on trust because, historically speaking, we cannot be absolutely sure.

c. 'Lives' of Jesus*

Mark was the first to write a life of Jesus. He used material which came to him through the early church and possibly, as we have seen, from people who had actually been with Jesus (a good reason for thinking that the events he records actually happened). Matthew was the next to write and he based his gospel on Mark's, copying large parts of it but also altering it in places and putting in a considerable amount of his own material, organising it all as he thought would best suit his purpose. What emerges is a very different picture of Jesus from Mark's and, again, we have to admit that we have learnt more about Matthew than about Jesus.

The same is true of Luke and John. Each tells the story of Jesus and in so doing gives himself and his own interests away. Since then, and right up to the present day, hundreds of people have written 'lives of Jesus', usually with the declared aim of getting back to the real facts about him. But they all have one thing in common – they tell us more about *themselves* than they do about Jesus. One person commenting on all these 'lives' said that it was as though each writer peered long and hard down a deep well searching frantically and then at the very bottom saw Jesus – a reflection of his *own* face in the water!

d. The contemporary Jesus

Why is it that Jesus is portrayed in so many different ways? Is it not possible to identify the character of Jesus? The answer it seems is 'no'. For one thing, as we have already noted, we cannot even be absolutely certain about the events of his life. When we carefully examine the evidence we do have (that is, the gospels), we find that each writer presents Jesus in his own particular way so that four differ-

* See chapter 1 d. for an explanation of the difference between 'gospel' and 'biography'.

ent portraits of Jesus emerge not one. The 'lives of Jesus' which have been written since the gospels, show us that Jesus is constantly being reinterpreted in people's minds. It seems that when someone comes to write about him they are influenced as much by the time and country in which they are living as they are by the historical evidence. For example, it was not too difficult for a Victorian writer to produce a Jesus who would have been at home in any nineteenth century English drawing room.

The Jesus of history has in fact become a *contemporary* figure with each generation reinterpreting him and his message in terms relevant to them and their situation.

It is not just the influences of time and culture, however, which determine the writer's eventual conclusions about Jesus. His own beliefs, ideas and prejudices also play a significant part. So it is perhaps not surprising to find that the revolutionary presents Jesus as a revolutionary, whilst the upholder of tradition finds that Jesus himself was really a traditionalist at heart.

Artists too have interpreted Jesus in many different ways. For some he is a king or an emperor, ruling the world; for others he is a suffering servant, dying an agonising death. In African art Jesus becomes an African, in Chinese art a Chinese man, and in European art he is presented as a European.

e. Your picture of Jesus

All this should act as something of a reminder to us. The picture of Jesus we have in our minds (and each of us has one even if we choose not to admit it), is largely one that we have constructed ourselves and is, therefore, unique. It will have been greatly influenced by the things we have been taught about him in the past (including the reading of this book!) and by personal experience. It is a picture that is probably in a constant state of change and it may tell us as much about ourselves as it does about Jesus.

144

f. Was there ever a real Jesus?

(i) Knowledge from outside the gospels

In view of what we have been saying it seems reasonable enough to ask, 'Was there ever a real Jesus?' In answer to that it must be said immediately that there can be very little doubt that Jesus was a real historical person. Apart from the evidence of the gospels and the letters of Paul, which were written even earlier than Mark, there is evidence outside the New Testament to confirm the existence of Jesus. We can quote at least four independent sources in support of this.

1. The Roman historian Tacitus (*c.* AD 115) writing about the persecution of Christians under Nero which followed the great fire in Rome in AD 64, said this,

> . . . Nero set up as the culprits and punished with the utmost refinements of cruelty a class hated for their abominations, who are commonly called Christians. Christus, from whom their name is derived, was executed at the hands of the procurator Pontius Pilate in the reign of Tiberius.

It is possible that Tacitus got his information about Pilate and the execution of Jesus from Roman records. He was certainly not writing to give confirmation that Jesus really had lived. In fact he was presumably not at all sympathetic to Christianity describing it as a 'pernicious superstition'.

2. Another Roman historian by the name of Suetonius also mentions Christians in connection with the events of AD 64, describing them as 'a set of men adhering to a novel and mischievous superstition'.

He also mentions some Jews who were expelled from Rome about AD 52 for ' . . continually making disturbances at the instigation of Chrestus' (presumably a different spelling of Christ). This probably refers to arguments which had occurred between Jews and Christians.

3. Some interesting correspondence has been preserved between a Roman called Pliny the Younger, who was ruler of Bithynia (part of modern day Turkey) about AD 112, and Trajan the Roman Emperor. Apparently Pliny was con-

cerned as to what action he should take concerning Christians, who had been banned in the Empire from practising their religion, so he wrote to Trajan for advice. He explained that it had so far been his policy to set free any who at his request cursed Christ because that was ' . . . a thing which, it is said, genuine Christians cannot be induced to do.' Others who would not give up their beliefs at Pliny's instruction were put to death, as much for their obstinacy as for their faith. Pliny had established that the Christians were guilty only of meeting together and reciting a hymn 'to Christ, as to a god'.

4. The fourth source is not quite as reliable. It is to be found in the writings of the Jewish historian, Josephus, and the passage which refers to Christ was probably altered by a Christian editor and is, therefore, biased in favour of Christianity. It speaks of Jesus as a wise man, a worker of marvellous deeds and a teacher. It speaks also of his death on the cross at the hands of Pilate and the Jewish authorities. Even if Josephus did not write this himself it seems likely that he had made some mention of Jesus and his death.

There are also some references to Jesus in Jewish religious writings of the time. These are nearly always hostile but do give further independent evidence of Jesus' existence as a historical person.

(ii) Knowledge from the gospels

As you can see, the information about Jesus which exists outside the New Testament is rather thin and uninformative and has, in the main, been recorded by those who were *against* Christianity. This strengthens the case that Jesus really lived because, if any of those writers had the slightest reason to doubt that Jesus had existed, they would have said so quite plainly. But they did not. In fact, in the case of Tacitus, we are given direct confirmation of the gospel account that Jesus was put to death on the order of Pontius Pilate.

Our main source of information about Jesus' life is still the gospels and, as we have seen in the case of Mark, they were written by people who had faith that Jesus was the Son of God. They wrote about Jesus of Nazareth who had been a great teacher and miracle worker and who had been put to death by the Romans. But they also had faith that Jesus was the Messiah. They believed that three days after his execution he had been raised by God. Death had been but a temporary set-back and through the resurrection a great victory over the powers of evil had been won. Jesus was alive again and with God. His faithful followers also felt his presence with them as they went about their daily lives. He was not physically with them, but it seemed to them that he was living in their hearts and minds. They were now Jesus' representatives on earth and it was up to them to do his work.

These beliefs coloured all that the gospel writers told about Jesus, and they did not hesitate to make what we might think to be fantastic claims on his behalf. As the Messiah (the Christ) Jesus could do anything.

g. Was Jesus God or man?

This is a question we do not propose to answer! We leave it to the individual reader to make up his or her own mind.

In traditional Christian teaching, Jesus is one of the three persons who make up the Trinity (the belief that God is three persons in one, Father, Son and Holy Spirit). As such he is God or as John describes him in the opening of his gospel, 'the Word' who existed from the beginning of creation, and who came to earth as Jesus and lived among men.

Matthew and Luke are the two gospel writers who tell us about Jesus' birth at Bethlehem. Their accounts stress that Jesus was God's son. He was born to a virgin who conceived as a result of the activity of God's Spirit. Matthew calls Jesus, 'Emmanuel', which means 'God with us'.

Mark begins his gospel with Jesus' baptism and the Old Testament language he uses (see chapter 5) suggests that at this point God adopted Jesus as his son. It was Mark's aim to stress that Jesus was the Messiah from the beginning of his ministry even though many people failed to recognise this.

As Christianity became more established, the idea developed that Jesus had, in fact, been both man and God. (This eventually became accepted teaching but not without much argument.) He was man, in that he experienced what it was like to live on earth with its temptations and sufferings, and he was God, in that he existed before and after his earthly life, and even while on earth had been sinless.

This idea has become the traditional teaching of the Christian church, but today not all people who could call themselves Christians hold to this belief. Many would prefer to regard Jesus simply as a man, albeit a very special and extraordinary man, who displayed god-like qualities and showed people what it meant to lead a good life trusting perfectly in God. In that sense he could truly be described as God's son. But they prefer not to think of him as God who came to live on earth.

If Jesus was simply a man, why do the gospel writers present him as though he were more than that? Were they deliberately out to deceive? It seems highly unlikely. What inspired them to write was their conviction that Jesus was the Christ. They believed implicitly that Jesus had risen from the dead. This was no normal human event and could only have been the work of God. All that they wrote was coloured by this overwhelming conviction, and they wrote with enthusiasm to pass on this good news to others. Where information about Jesus' life was lacking they referred to the Old Testament for guidance. After all, it was here that the coming of the Messiah was prophesied. In the Old Testament they found what they believed must be references to Jesus. Stories about miraculous births, details of the Suffering Servant and so on. In telling the story of Jesus as they did, it was not their intention to mislead but to record the truth as they saw it.

When we read the gospels today we must accept that we may find some of the ideas which they express hard to believe. This is not surprising because the outlook of twentieth century people is so different from the outlook of people who lived in the first century. When we try to answer Jesus' own question, 'Who do you say I am?', we do so with all the knowledge that we, as twentieth century people, possess.

So, to be Christians today, do we have to accept all that Mark tells us, or should we use his gospel as a source of information about Jesus to help us to arrive at *our own* answer – just as Mark himself used his sources to help him to arrive at his conclusions?

Many twentieth century Christians find it possible to have faith in Jesus and try to live as he taught, without believing literally in everything the gospels tell us about him.

When you answer Jesus' question (and whether you are a Christian or not you still hold some opinion about him) how much of Mark's answer will you make your own?

Questions for chapter 14

1. What difficulties do we face when we come to study the lives of people of the past? Do these same difficulties apply to a study of Jesus' life?

2. What picture of Jesus do you have in your mind? What has influenced your ideas about him?

3. What evidence is there outside the gospels to confirm that Jesus really did live?

4. Do you prefer to think of Jesus as God or man?

Books for reference or further study

For students

C. F. D. Moule, *The Gospel According to Mark*, Cambridge University Press.
D. Cupitt and P. Armstrong, *Who was Jesus?*, BBC Publications.
Student's Bible Atlas, Lutterworth Press.

For teachers

D. E. Nineham, *St. Mark*, Pelican New Testament Commentaries.
C. F. Evans, *The Beginning of the Gospel*, S.P.C.K.
J. Robinson, *The Problem of History in Mark*, SCM Press.
J. M. Hull, *Hellenistic Magic and the Synoptic Tradition*, SCM Press.

Index of Biblical References